MARKKANEN
SAN FRANCISCO
11-30-90

SETTING FREE
THE ACTOR

D0037418

SETTING FREE THE ACTOR

OVERCOMING CREATIVE BLOCKS

ANN BREBNER

MERCURY HOUSE
San Francisco, California

Copyright © 1990 by Ann Brebner

Published in the United States by
Mercury House
San Francisco, California

Distributed to the trade by
Consortium Book Sales & Distribution, Inc.
St. Paul, Minnesota

All rights reserved, including, without limitation, the right of the publisher to
sell directly to end users of this and other Mercury House books. No part of
this book may be reproduced in any form or by any electronic or mechanical
means, including information storage and retrieval systems, without permission in writing from the publisher, except by a reviewer who may quote brief
passages in a review.

Mercury House and colophon are registered trademarks
of Mercury House, Incorporated

Manufactured in the United States of America

Library of Congress Cataloging-in-Publication Data

Brebner, Ann, 1923–
  Setting free the actor : overcoming creative blocks / by Ann Brebner.
    p.   cm.
  ISBN 0–916515–80–X : $10.95
  1. Acting—Psychological aspects.   2. Self-realization.   I. Title.
PN2071.P78B7   1990
792'.028'019—dc20   90–5875
                                                             CIP

For my sons, Alexander and Jay

Contents

Acknowledgments

Every actor and director I have worked with has in some way contributed to this book. I am grateful that I have been privileged to have them in my life.

Certainly Michel St. Denis, who headed the Old Vic Theatre School in London, exerted a profound influence over me and my feelings toward actors. Michel was the first person in whom I was aware of an unquenchable curiosity; I owe him endless thanks for encouraging me to retain my own.

In my journey through the unfamiliar process of writing a book, I was supported by many dear friends in the theater and film worlds who read version after version of various chapters, offering encouragement, opinions, and advice when they were sorely needed. Among those friends are Susan O'Connell; Robert Egan, Chair of Drama at the University of California at Santa Barbara; Dr. Joan Kenley; Greg Winfield; Anne Lamott; Dana Evans; Jonathan Zeichner; Frances Hill; Dr. Otto Vanoni; and Sid Ganis. My heartfelt thanks to all of them, and to my extended family unmentioned by name, for their encouragement as the book inched its way into life.

For providing a hospitable work environment, I am deeply indebted to Jo Farrell of J F Talent, Inc. in Denver, where the "Denver Experiment" took place. My sincere thanks also to

Kathleen Marsh and to Maureen and Christine Farrell for their valuable support and all the good times.

At Mercury House, my thanks to Alev Lytle Croutier for her belief in the book, to Carol Costello for creating shape out of shapelessness, to Alison Macondray for her "caringness" toward me and the book, to Dayna Macy for her enthusiasm, to Jessie Wood for her fine eye, and especially to Nancy Palmer Jones for her editing and her understanding of the spirit and soul of the actor.

Without the opportunity to work with my clients this book could not have happened; to them I owe a debt of gratitude for their truth and inspiration.

Ann Brebner
San Rafael, California
February 1990

prologue
An Actor's Journey

Everyone, from time to time, trips over unfinished emotional business from the past. For those of us who are actors, these stumbling blocks have a profound effect on the quality of our work and on our ability to develop our craft to its greatest state of grace.

This book is about making peace with our emotional heritage and taking adult responsibility for our own creative life. Sir Laurence Olivier always referred to acting as "my work." I like that phrase because it gives an appropriate dignity, reality, and importance to what we do. With each project we undertake — and that includes working on ourselves and our creative blocks — we are fulfilling one segment of a lifelong commitment to our creativity. Coming to terms with our emotional history is as much a part of "our work" as going to classes, interviewing, auditioning, and giving performances. All are part of the journey we undertake to find our own unique means of self-expression.

In my own journey, I have been blessed with many experiences that seem designed to support the work described in this book. My father wanted me to be a doctor, and I had been accepted to medical school. I wanted to specialize in psychiatry. I already had a bachelor's degree in abnormal psychology, but my secret dream was to do something "special" — to be a pianist, or an actress, or a director. When I won a New Zealand government scholarship to study theater in Europe and gained admission to the Old Vic Theatre School, I felt that I had been handed the world on a silver platter. All thoughts of medical school were thrown to the wind.

I wore a suit on my first day at the school, and so did several of the other students. But that was the only time we did. We learned from the ground up — wiring the theater, creating lighting plans, installing and running the lights, stage managing, designing sets and costumes, and watching in horror as the shop crew built scenery to our off-scale drawings. Some of that scenery wouldn't even fit through the scene-shop doors. We were to develop into directors who knew all the technical skills and who understood firsthand what could be done and what could not.

Some of my most vivid memories are of Michel St. Denis, who was the head of the school and would later head up Juilliard at Lincoln Center in New York. Michel had directed Sir Laurence Olivier in *Oedipus Rex,* the play that made Olivier famous. They were friends, and Olivier sometimes visited the school.

Michel always called us "dear chap" in his French accent; it didn't matter whether we were male or female. As long as he called us "dear chap," things could be said to be going well. But when he called us "Mr." or "Miss," we prepared for squalls.

I can still hear Michel's voice saying, "What is the truth of the moment, dear chap? The truth!" and then pushing and pushing until he got me to give him the very heart of what was happening. He seemed to get there so directly, while the path was so tortuous for me at first.

The school was all-consuming; we worked from nine in the morning until midnight. It was the most wonderful, fulfilling, infuriating, difficult, exhilarating time in my life. I belonged to a vital family the like of which I had never known; the loving, demanding, disciplining, and indulgent father was Michel.

Throughout my adult life I have been involved in either theater or film. I have cofounded a Shakespeare festival, directed many of Shakespeare's plays, guest lectured at Stanford, directed in New York, worked as a casting director on many films, presented workshops for actors, and acted as agent for Danny Glover, Peter Coyote, Bill Irwin, Joanna Cassidy, Joe Spano, Kathleen Quinlan, Max Gail, Peter Donat, and David Dukes. And I have marveled at the miracles that actors perform every day.

Although my training in psychology was put aside when I chose a career in the theater, I have always remained vitally interested in what goes on under the surface for all people, and particularly for artists. Some of the greatest rewards of my work as an agent have been the personal relationships I have formed with actors. I found long ago that I had an ability to recognize when something in an actor's life was affecting his or her work. I could tell what was going on by watching readings and taped auditions, by directing the actor on tape, or by listening to feedback from directors and casting directors. The conversations that sprang from these observations were always productive and opened up new vistas for my clients and for me. Chapter One tells the story of how these conversations led to the work described in this book.

To me actors are not defined by racial origin; neither should casting be so defined. Accordingly I have not identified any clients racially, in the hope that readers of all races will be able to associate themselves intimately with the case histories.

If I have a mission today, it is to send actors into the twenty-first century with strength and security in the dignity of their work. The exercises, tools, and tasks in this book have been developed over the years through my work with clients and are well within the reach of any actor. Each of my clients has taught me something precious and unique. I thank them for their courage in sharing their most dearly held secrets and fears and for the great joy that working with them has brought me. As much as this book may be mine, it is also theirs.

part one

The Blocks
to Creativity

Acting is a vehicle, a means for self study; self exploration; a possibility of salvation. The actor has himself as a field of work. His head, his eye, his ear, and his heart are what he is studying, and what he is studying with.

Peter Brook, *The Empty Space*

chapter 1
The Journey Begins

As actors, we work with every facet of ourselves. Our tools are not just words but also our minds, bodies, voices, faces, movements, emotions, inspiration, and imagination — often, it seems, our very souls.

Cameras and theater audiences pick up every nuance of what is within us — rapture, anger, grief, love. They also note any hint of self-consciousness, defensiveness, or pretense. On film or onstage, what we intend to convey can sometimes be obscured by what we do *not* intend to convey. This means that our work may be more vulnerable to unfinished emotional business than other people's — even other artists'. And it means that, if we wish to do our work with a sense of freedom and joy, we must face the challenge of dissolving our old fears, angers, and hurts so that they no longer control us. Through this healing process, we find a sense of certainty and wholeness within ourselves that we may have thought was lost forever.

Our most painful and exhilarating moments as actors come when we are asked to go into our deepest feelings in order to find or create a character. This is the journey on which we're embarking in this book, and the character we will discover is ourselves.

My Work with Actors

Since 1985, I have been helping actors reconnect with their creative center, the center where the desire to act is born.

I remember sitting at my desk in San Francisco, about eighteen months before I sold my agency to begin this new work, looking out across the bay and thinking about a particular actor. Adam had read for a costarring role in a film, and I had been sure that he would get it. But he had not been cast, and I think I felt as disappointed as he did.

The casting director had not been impressed with Adam's interview and reading, but I knew that Adam was a wonderful actor and that he should have been able to audition well. And a similar thing had happened the week before; Adam had not been cast in a part I had been sure he would get. What was going on?

I had been working with actors for decades—directing them, acting as their agent, talking with them, watching them day by day—and I was keenly aware not only that actors are subject to some painful problems and stresses but also that their work is particularly vulnerable to the emotional blocks they put up to protect themselves from pain. As I sat there thinking about Adam, I wondered idly whether anyone had ever set out to work with actors on their unique problems and stresses, to examine how and why the blocks were first put in place and what could be done to remove them. Wouldn't that be interesting work, I mused.

I tried to put the thought out of my mind, but over the next several months it kept returning and returning, and eventually I started asking a few people what they thought of the idea. Slowly I began to help actors solve their problems. At first these problems were mostly prosaic ones—the politics or logistics of being cast in a certain role, for instance—but it always seemed that there was something beyond these practical matters that actors wanted to talk about.

They said things like:

• "I'm addicted to 'perfect,' 'best,' and I have a hard time with this as an actress. I'm always judging myself."

- "I get called back on interviews, but I don't know why, so I don't know how to decide what to do."
- "I feel that I'm an impostor a lot of the time, even though I know I'm well trained and well prepared."
- "I go blank in interviews. Sometimes I can't even hear what is being said."
- "I feel 'they' know something bad about me, or that by mistake I'll tell them something bad."
- "I don't know what they want me to do."
- "If I only knew who they wanted me to be . . ."
- "I get cast and I never know why. So I'm always anxious when I'm working."

When these actors realized that they had a safe place where they could talk about their problems, they began to blossom. I was one of the few people they knew who understood the realities of their daily lives yet had no financial stake in their success. I wasn't relating to them as agent, director, producer, or casting director. I wasn't depending on what they did or didn't do for my success, but I did know firsthand about the problems they faced.

These actors had rarely had a chance to talk with someone who cared only about how they felt, someone with whom they could be vulnerable and admit to feeling confused, unsuccessful, and victimized, or, on the other hand, delighted with how things were going. They didn't have to play any roles with me, pretending to be either strong and confident or needy and subservient, and this gave them the freedom to reveal both the darker and the lighter sides of themselves.

Most of these actors felt that something was standing between them and success, causing them to sabotage themselves and preventing them from expressing, enjoying, and sharing their work. They felt cut off from their creative center—the part of themselves that gave them inspiration, freedom, expressiveness, and joy. Instead, they felt frustration, anger, depression, and guilt. The more I listened to these actors, the more I understood that behind their immediate problems were deeper issues that governed or controlled their actions, producing unwanted results. But how were we to reach those deeper issues?

Sometimes in my talks with these first clients, I would catch a glimpse of a magical person. When I asked about the client's hopes and dreams, the magic was not there; but when I asked what his or her dreams had been *as a child,* then the actor's whole being would glow. This was the clue I needed. Each actor's connection to the child that he or she had been proved to be the path down which we could journey toward an understanding of the deeper issues.

When these actors began removing blocks and reconnecting with their creative center, everything seemed to work. Difficulties became creative challenges. They felt a powerful, effortless commitment to their work and a measure of control over what they were doing. I could see their faces change the instant they realized that they could return to that place of trust and inspiration, the place where they felt most real and alive. They looked a bit like the remarkable children they had been, as if they had come home to themselves.

I love solving problems. I have always loved puzzles, and in a way each client was a new puzzle. If I sat still long enough and listened carefully enough, the core of the problem usually revealed itself. It wasn't always a comfortable revelation, but with my clients' courage and my own patience, we usually made it to the other side of the problem.

My uncle, on whose farm I spent summers as a child in New Zealand, used to say to me, "If you ever get lost, don't run around crazy. You'll know where to go when you know where to go. The longer you stay in one place, the more you'll know about where you are. You'll know where the sun rises and sets, and so you'll know which is north and south and east and west."

My uncle's wisdom gave me a kind of peace. I learned from him to stay with discomfort until I knew it. When I had understood it for what it was, then I could deal with it and leave it. The time spent with my uncle was a golden part of my childhood. I use his wisdom often when I'm working with clients.

"So, Why Are We Here?"

This is the first question I ask each new client. Sooner or later, it becomes clear that we're here to release old hurts, old angers, and old fears so that we can make peace with our emotional past and learn to nurture the creativity that our profession demands.

We're here to remove whatever obstacles or inhibitions are in the way of that vulnerability with which cameras and audiences have love affairs. We're here to minimize the fear, the self-doubts, and the internal editing so that we can feel free to be adventurous, spontaneous, and impulsive. We are not here to "fix" ourselves or to make ourselves more "normal." An artist friend always has to remind her eye doctor that she does not *want* twenty-twenty vision. She needs to see well enough to drive safely and to read, but she wants to paint the leaves on a tree as *she* sees them, not necessarily as they actually are. Just so, an actor needs to release his or her own unique, fascinating, and idiosyncratic self.

In short, we're here to rediscover the center where the desire, the energy, and the ideas for our creative expression are generated. This is the buoyant, unself-conscious part of us that led us, as children, to act on our creative impulses. If we had an idea for a play about a princess and a treasure, we strung up some blankets on a rope, made an entrance, and *did the play* without stopping to worry about whether it was any good, or whether our craft was perfect enough, or whether it would make money, or whether the critics would praise it.

The creative center is the source of our work at its spontaneous best. We know this center when we touch it or when we see, hear, or feel others touch it in themselves. And we are working from that creative center when we feel the thrill of bringing what is inside us out into the world and seeing other people respond to it.

As actors, we must be strong enough to be vulnerable, and we must be prepared to reencounter our own deepest feelings, even if the memories they evoke are painful. This book is about facing these challenges with courage and grace. It is about:

- Pinpointing exactly when and why we cut ourselves off from our creative center.
- Finding our way back to that creative center, using the tools and exercises that I have developed through my work with actors.
- Developing support systems that keep us focused and moving forward.
- Trusting our instincts and learning to live at peace with ourselves and our talents.

These tasks should not be undertaken lightly. They require commitment and a willingness to experience discomfort and to seek further help when it is needed. I don't "treat" people in my work; I help them identify problems and encourage them to seek whatever help they feel is appropriate — for example, individual therapy, support groups, or organizations such as Adult Children of Alcoholics.

These tasks also require a willingness to change. My client Jim taught me how important such willingness is. He was not an actor, but he held a responsible position in a large corporation and often spoke to large groups to solicit business for his company. He came to me because he felt that he needed to create greater warmth and rapport with his audiences.

After we had spent some time together, I videotaped one of his speeches. On this tape, the warm and friendly person with whom I had been talking disappeared; in his place was someone remote and impersonal. It was obvious that Jim did not like asking these people for their business. In fact, I sensed that he despised them.

"Do you actually despise these people?" I asked. He paused a moment, then answered, "Yes, I do." I pointed out that trying to seduce people into liking you and buying your service when you actually despise them is an uphill battle at best, and probably a lost cause. Even if you succeed, which is unlikely, you will have betrayed both them and yourself. My client was in trouble, as a performer and as a person.

As we started to probe these personal and professional issues, Jim began to resist my questions. He simply did not want to look at these areas. He spent considerable time outlining to me the complexities of his life, explaining that he couldn't possibly change any part of it because if he did, everything would fall apart. "I know you're going to ask me to change some parts of what I do," he said, "and I just have to tell you that I can't change anything."

This was a moment of truth. Jim had flown in from the East Coast especially for two full days of meetings with me. Did I have the courage to say that, if he didn't want to change, then I couldn't work with him, since change was implicit in my work? Or would I pretend tó be productive in some other way?

I told him the truth, and our meeting ended on a note of honesty and mutual respect. I later heard that someone had asked him whether the sessions had been valuable, and he had answered, "They were worth a million dollars." He had told himself a basic truth: He wasn't willing to change. He told me later that making this statement had enabled him to understand what was wrong. He promised himself that eventually he would deal with his problems. Whatever Jim may have learned, however, I learned far more.

Change can be painful and difficult, but without it we can't get to the magic that lies at our creative center.

The Child We Left Behind

Time and again, actors begin sessions with statements like:

- "My acting teacher tells me to let go and have fun. I don't know how to do that."
- "I don't want to go back to my childhood. It was awful, yet I feel there is some stuff there that I need."
- "I grew up as an isolated only child. I'm really afraid of showing emotion or being physically close to someone. I love acting, but I can't keep doing it and still avoid that kind of vulnerability."

Most of my clients feel that they cut themselves off from their feelings at some point during childhood or adolescence. At that moment of decision, when all that mattered was sheer emotional survival, they left behind the child they had been. Many faced difficult circumstances in their formative years. I don't think that we actors are any more likely than other people to have had abusive or traumatic childhoods, but I do believe that, if these events have not been healed, they are highly likely to affect our work.

I've learned from my clients that the blocks to creativity come not from the traumatic events themselves but from the fact that in order to survive the traumatic events, we had to cut ourselves off from our feelings and our creative center. These traumatic events can be anything from physical or emotional abuse, divorce, a parent's alcoholism, or the death of a loved one to an offhand comment from parents, peers, or even strangers that was never meant to hurt—but did.

When we heard that thoughtless remark or experienced that unjust punishment, our instinctive response was to throw up barriers against the hurt, cutting us off from our feelings. Without access to our feelings, we put our creativity on hold or channeled it into daydreams or secret fantasies.

No matter how good our barriers are, however, some hurt always seeps through. Rather than acknowledge it, we're inclined to throw up more barriers. We become clowns, devil-may-care risk takers, show-offs, angry rebels, substance abusers, anguished or defiant outcasts. Or we find more subtle ways of sabotaging ourselves and our work. Because we are so inventive, the list is almost endless.

We are the only ones who can remove those barriers, and the freedom and exhilaration we experience after working with these events from our past are worth the initial pain of going back to them. Once we eliminate those blocks, the work of acting can go forward.

As actors, we need to be able to call on everything that is within us. We need a playful, off-the-wall quality in our work. We can't be afraid to play rebellious or antagonistic characters to the edge. We can never fuse with another character or abandon our character's agenda to another actor's. We need to be able to love without merging, to be angry without feeling either dangerous or endangered.

In Chapter Three, we will explore ways of going back to get the child we left behind, of healing that child and reparenting him or her in ways that foster love rather than fear.

Identifying Our Moments of Decision

What kinds of things might cause us to throw up barriers and shut down our feelings?

Perhaps we had a parent who saw the budding actor stringing up blankets for a play in the garage and asked, "What makes you think you're so special?" or said, "Don't get foolish ideas in your head." It might have been a room full of other five-year-olds or several uncles and aunts who laughed at the little actress clomping downstairs in her mommy's high-heeled shoes. I know several child actors who were teased mercilessly when they returned to school after shooting a movie. Two of them stopped acting because they couldn't stand being considered "different" and being treated as if they didn't belong.

We all want approval, not ridicule. As children, we often believe that our very survival depends on being liked and accepted. We will do anything in order to survive, so we deny and shut down those deep, creative parts of ourselves that make us feel "different." At certain nightmarish moments, we give up our dreams in order to fit in and earn approval. We want those other people on our side, and we will hide our light if that's what it takes to get them there.

Such moments occur whenever we decide that our feelings — or the expression of them — have gotten us in trouble and caused pain, despair, rejection, or a sense of being misunderstood. We never want to experience those things again, so we decide: *My feelings betray me; therefore, I will not feel.*

Sometimes these moments are delayed. We are told, "Go ahead and get your degree, and *then* you can think about becoming an actress — if you still want to." The implications are that acting is unimportant, foolish, or at best secondary and that we will probably grow out of such a ridiculous and pretentious ambition.

Some parents may attend all of their daughter's school performances and are delighted to bask in the reflected glory of her minor stardom. But when she graduates and announces her intention to be a professional actress on Broadway, the father declares, "No daughter of *mine* is going to be an actress."

The daughter is surprised and confused. She feels as if she's been encouraged down a path and then abandoned. In order to preserve her relationship with her parents, she may give up her dream. She may come to agree with what they say about actresses being second-class people, or about her having no real talent, or about how difficult it is to succeed as an actress, or about people in the theater not living "normal" lives. She may betray herself in order to conform, to fit in, to be accepted and loved, and to retain her parents' approval.

These moments of giving up the dream don't always relate directly to our work itself; they can have to do with how we see ourselves and the world around us.

All his life, my client Dan has been in second place. Now he is too frequently second choice in casting decisions, and he feels trapped in this "always-a-bridesmaid" syndrome. When we looked back to see where the pattern might have started, Dan remembered a time he had come in first. He was ten years old and had won a junior tennis tournament. He remembers raising the trophy over his head and smiling up at the crowd. He felt sure his father would be pleased. But his father didn't speak to him the whole way home. Finally, as they were getting out of the car, he turned to Dan and said tightly, "Nobody likes a smug winner."

Dan interpreted that statement to mean "Nobody likes you when you win." That may or may not have been what his father intended, but it was the judgment Dan made at the time and the standard by which he had lived his life since that moment.

A single statement can prompt decisions that last a lifetime. When Joan's sister "ran off" at sixteen to live with her boyfriend, write songs, and play the guitar, their mother told Joan, "I hope you never disappoint us like your sister did." Joan had already begun a career as an actress, but she interpreted her mother's statement to mean that it would please her family if she married instead of "disgracing" them as her sister had. Since marriage meant approval, at age eighteen Joan entered into a disastrous and abusive marriage with her first boyfriend. After the wedding, she went to college and continued to study acting. Once again, two unrelated situations became linked in her mind. Having what she most wanted, acting, became associated with the pain and abuse of her marriage.

At twenty-eight, she is beginning to unravel what happened. She understands for the first time how her sister's leaving home affected her life, realizes that she drew some mistaken conclusions, and is beginning to straighten things out. She is now married to a supportive man, employed by a large corporation, back in acting classes, rediscovering the old feelings and excitement, and much happier, even though she no longer intends to make acting her career.

Linda is a successful Broadway actress. She could be even more successful, but she always seems to sabotage herself when the really big roles come along, doing things like flying off to Paris instead of staying in New York for the callback.

All through high school, Linda played lead roles in school shows. Her father had died when she was four, and she and her mother were very close — in fact, Linda remembers the closeness as being stifling, especially in the area of her career. As high school graduation approached, her mother stepped up the campaign for Linda to go to a local midwestern college, where she could live at home, and become a teacher.

For the first time, Linda and her mother found themselves in strong disagreement. Linda was already in the process of enrolling in a New York acting school. She left for New York in a flood of tears and swamped with guilt, her mother's words ringing in her ears: "If you are successful, I'll know you are a whore!"

Over the years, they patched up their relationship and got along fairly well as long as no one mentioned Linda's career, but three years ago Linda's mother injured herself and Linda went back to the Midwest to be with her for two months. They had some bitter conversations, and when Linda returned to New York her behavior became more and more self-destructive. Her agent had several serious talks with her, and her friends became concerned.

This was when Linda came to see me. She already knew that she was extremely angry with her mother. In our second session together, she said that she was secretly afraid that her mother might be right — that if she got the leading role for which she had auditioned, she would suddenly turn into a bad person. She might not literally be a whore, but she would feel guilty and ashamed of things she'd done, especially of leaving her mother.

Once that was out, she was able to pinpoint exactly why she was behaving erratically. She felt, at a deep level, that it was dangerous for her to become successful.

Over the next year, Linda worked hard with a therapist to deal with her anger. She finally forgave her mother; now, when they spend time together, Linda feels free to talk about her work. She has minimized her fear of success and is back on track.

Until we have dealt with the past, as these clients are beginning to do, we will keep recreating the same situations over and over. The cast of characters may be new, and the external circumstances may be different, but the substance of the situation will be the same. The role of the teacher, parent, or football coach may be taken by a casting director or a producer, the curtain strung up on a rope may become an audition, but the emotional material will be the same.

When we've gone back and confronted old patterns, they begin to slip away, and we can start creating new and more productive dramas.

Forgiving the Past

The people who prompted these moments of decision usually did so with the best intentions. Our parents, for example, learned to parent from their own father and mother, and probably repeated whatever was done to them. Most of what they did, they did out of love — but that doesn't mean it worked. A mother may have encouraged her daughter to conform in order to spare her pain, but the result was that the daughter gave up her dreams and became a resentful, unfulfilled, unhappy woman.

We don't have classes in parenting in our society, and parents often act as much out of fear as love. Children don't always get the trust that nurtures creativity — or the time, or the unconditional love and acceptance, or the permission just to be themselves. Seldom, in present-day homes, are loving grandparents or great uncles and aunts available with limitless understanding and encouragement.

Nor do parents always remember that each of us is different. Some of us are apples and others are oranges, but many of us have had to learn to live in ways that are completely unnatural to us. When we announced firmly, "But I'm an apple," we may have received an answer suggesting that we would be wiser to pretend that we were oranges than to pursue the essence of our appleness. We did not understand why, but it seemed to be important to our parents or teachers.

Apples don't look, smell, or taste like oranges. An apple that tries to impersonate an orange or conform to the way oranges do things will not meet with much happiness or success.

Still, it doesn't do any good to carry around anger or resentment against our parents for how they "ruined" us. In most cases, our parents were just doing their best to protect and guide us, no matter how misinformed or disastrous the results may have been. Holding onto resentment doesn't change the past or produce positive results in the present or future. The sooner we can let go of it, the better off we'll be.

We must forgive ourselves as well. Whatever we did, even shutting down our connection with the creative center, we did in order to survive emotionally. The events in our lives were so traumatic, or *felt* so traumatic, that at the time we had no alternative. We just wanted to belong and be loved. We didn't realize that it was acceptable to be unique, creative individuals who didn't necessarily conform to the world around us. We didn't know that we could embrace all of ourselves. And we didn't know what shutting down would cost us.

We were like the small matagouri bush that grows in New Zealand. It is an ancient species, and it will do anything in order to survive. It grows in almost any climate—wherever the winds, the birds, or the fates send it—but it alters its form and appearance dramatically to adapt to different surroundings.

In dry, windswept regions, the matagouri is dark gray with hard thorns and only a few rudimentary, grayish leaves. It looks dead, but if you try to break a twig you find that it is alive and tough. Where it gets more rain and better soil, the little bush flourishes. Its thorns become green and flexible, and it grows thick, shiny, green leaves.

Near one of my favorite places in New Zealand, a gray-brown matagouri clings to the top of a rocky, windswept outcropping. At the base of the forty-foot cliff, another little bush is green and lush because it happens to sit near the water.

Like the matagouri, creative people manage to survive in even the most inhospitable environments. We can adapt to a lack of nurturing, believing that this is the way it has to be, but even the smallest amount of encouragement can reverse the situation and allow us to flourish. As adults, our job is to make sure we get that support and nurturing.

Responding to the Creative Imperative

No matter how cut off we feel from our creative center, the time will come when we can't ignore the need to express ourselves, a time when it is more painful and frustrating *not* to express our creativity than to risk going back, finding the pain, and healing it. Once we have healed the old hurts, we can take all the energy we've been using to conceal them and apply it to our work.

First there was the ecstasy: "I want to act!" Then there was the agony of shutting down and throwing up barriers. On the journey back through that agony to the ecstasy, we have to face those painful moments when we felt foolish, or stupid, or bad, or as if everyone else knew something that we didn't.

We want to run from that kind of pain, but at some point we have to stop running. Until we face those old fears, every other success we have in life—good relationships, children, financial security, even spiritual fulfillment—will be followed by a small "Yeah, but . . ." in our minds.

Going back to look at those experiences without shutting down again is tremendously empowering. Reconnecting with our creative center is like coming home to ourselves. On the day I followed my feelings and chose, against my father's wishes, to attend the Old Vic Theatre School rather than medical school, I felt extremely anxious. What if I had made a mistake? How would I know? Four months later, when I actually walked into the building where I was to spend the next year, I felt that I *belonged* there. It was like taking a bath in warm oil or jumping into a feather bed. Finally, I belonged to myself again, and that feeling is reborn each time I act, direct, produce, or do anything that brings me back to the experience of choosing and living for *me*.

Trusting Our Instincts

Coming home to ourselves usually means a shift in focus from the left brain to the right brain—that is, it means settling into a place where our thoughts and actions are no longer controlled, edited, and planned but are intuitive, instinctive, and trustworthy. The left side of the brain is good at things like balancing the checkbook; it knows when we are late, can plan for next year or even next century, is good at deductive reasoning, and controls our conscious memory. It also routes information and instructions throughout the body and to other parts of the brain. In some senses, it is a brilliant traffic cop. The right side of the brain deals with feelings, color, design, shape, sound, and concepts; it has access to the unconscious. As actors, we need to release and embrace this right-brain part of ourselves—the intuitive, feeling-oriented, integrative, instinctive aspect of our being.

Early in most actors' training, there is a lot of left-brain work. Many things need to be learned and understood. The nuts and bolts of the business of acting require left-brain attention. Learning lines, remembering blocking, working on the intention of a scene, figuring out the subtext, making decisions about a hundred details—all of these things and more have to be consciously learned and assimilated.

At some point, though, we have to trust that all the programming we've done in the left brain will work—that we will remember our lines and hit our marks—and that we just need to let go. Then the right brain can join in and unleash its inspiration and creativity. The first few times we engage the creative right brain, we feel as if we may explode. This feeling of excitement and of being "on the edge" never disappears entirely—we wouldn't want it to—but we do learn to trust it more and more.

When the left brain and right brain are functioning together—that is, when each hemisphere is accomplishing its own work and is supporting and communicating with the other, rapidly and effortlessly—then we are able to work at our creative best. But when stress of any sort is introduced, the communication between the two hemispheres slows down. Under extreme stress it ceases altogether, leaving the left brain in charge and chattering noisily at us, demanding that we do things "right," that we be "perfect." Perhaps such stress arises because a current situation reminds us, on a deep level, of some traumatic event in our past. The choice we made then—to cut off our feelings and to survive by making conscious and careful decisions about what is right and what is wrong—allowed the left brain to take over. This is the same "solution" that today blocks our access to the right brain, that intuitive side of ourselves from which good acting comes. Our journey back to ourselves will teach us new ways to handle the stresses of our profession and will help us to reclaim the freedom that acting demands.

chapter 2
The Actor from a
Dysfunctional Family

Not all actors grow up in dysfunctional families, but the information we now have about such families can shed light on all kinds of psychological blocks that begin in childhood.

Dysfunctional families are not just those in which abuse or alcoholism is present; they include any family in which people are not free to be or to express themselves naturally and honestly. For actors, such restrictions present special problems, and a whole cluster of blocks frequently occurs for those of us who have grown up in dysfunctional homes.

When old issues born in our dysfunctional families have not been healed, we are likely to recreate relationships from our past with people in our lives now, such as other actors, directors, producers, and casting directors.

In this chapter, we look at some of the possible consequences of growing up in a dysfunctional home. Much of the material included here is derived from the work of Adult Children of Alcoholics (ACA), an organization to which I have referred a number of clients and for which I have the greatest admiration.

What Is a Dysfunctional Family?

For the purposes of this book, we will say that a dysfunctional family is one that doesn't work for one or more of the following reasons:

- At least one member of the family is addicted to a destructive substance (such as alcohol or other drugs) or to a destructive behavior (such as gambling, overspending, or overeating).
- There is physical or verbal abuse or violence.
- Love and approval are withheld as punishment.
- Children have to earn love and approval in virtually impossible ways.
- Children are not honored simply for being who they are, and their imagination and creative brilliance are stifled.
- Trauma is created by, for example, divorce, death, or frequent changes in location. (These traumas may also occur in healthy families, but they are treated as a part of life and incorporated into an essentially loving and stable environment. In dysfunctional families, they are not dealt with openly and so take on greater weight and start to control the lives of family members.)
- Parents relate to children in ways that are erratic or unpredictable.
- Promises are never kept.
- The relationships between family members are poorly defined and change at the whim of the parent. (One day a child may be treated as a slave and the next as a best friend. The child looks to the parent for a role definition in order to know how to behave.)
- There is little to be gained by telling the truth.
- People are not free to be themselves and to express their own truths, and they must maintain false facades.

These situations are difficult for anyone, but they present special challenges to young actors, who are apt to behave differently from other children, who have higher needs for creative expression, and who need at least as much unconditional love and acceptance as other children.

The Outside Versus the Inside View of the Dysfunctional Family

There are fundamental differences between the healthy family and the dysfunctional family. In a healthy family, what we see on the outside is very close to what is actually going on inside. If people seem happy, they probably *are* basically happy. If there are problems, we sense that something is wrong. No heroic efforts are made to hide the truth of what is happening.

This is not true in the dysfunctional family. The dysfunctional family presents to the world a porcelain-perfect, carefully painted facade. No cracks or blemishes are apparent when the dysfunctional family attends church together, cheers at the kids' soccer games, or goes on Sunday picnics. But on the inside, everyone's stomach is churning.

Every family member subscribes to the lie that things are fine. No one reveals the inner turmoil to friends, relatives, counselors, or ministers because the truth is so frightening, because they don't want to be "traitors" to the family conspiracy, and because children often sense that they would be thrown out of the family entirely if they told anyone the truth. The whole house of cards—the deceptions, lies, and cover-ups that hold the family together—could come crashing down if the truth were told.

Perhaps Daddy is an alcoholic and has violent bursts of temper, alternately beating the kids and buying them extravagant presents. Maybe Mom is jealous of her daughters' youth and beauty and goes out of her way to damage their self-esteem. Maybe son Jason has a problem with cocaine that no one is addressing.

If Jason seeks help with his coke problem, or if it comes out that his dad is violent when he's drunk, there will be no place for Jason in the family. If daughter Judy suggests that her mother is anything but the smiling, cookie-baking, nurturing lady she pretends to be, things will get even worse. If Mom herself tries to find help from a therapist, if Dad starts going to Alcoholics

Anonymous meetings, they will be admitting that something is wrong — and that's not allowed.

If anyone talks to a friend or seeks help, he or she will upset the delicate balance within the family and will suffer the consequences. What passes for love and acceptance will be withdrawn. No one can acknowledge a problem, so no one can find solutions.

In many cases, the children don't even realize that anything is wrong. They have always lived in this dysfunctional way and are conditioned to believe that this is just the way life is. For actors who come from dysfunctional families, this means that it is familiar, almost normal, to have things appear perfect on the outside but be chaotic within. This is not a condition that fosters good, productive work.

When we begin to heal the past, the idea that we could feel the same inside and out, and that we could feel secure in that state, is new, and it seems quite strange at first — it feels almost like a betrayal of the rest of the family. But this freedom to be honest is what gives us access to *all* our feelings, allows us to relate on a profound level to others, and enables us to respond to others with integrity. In inspired acting, there is no room for hiding and pretense.

Which Box Am I in Today?

In healthy families, the roles that people play are generally well defined, but they are also flexible enough to accommodate changing circumstances. For instance, if a mother gets sick and has to depend on the children to take care of her and the house for a few days, she is simply a sick mother who needs some caretaking at this particular time. She does not try to turn the children into her permanent parents, as might happen in a dysfunctional family. She is still the mother, and they are still her children. They know it and she knows it. They may be afraid because their mother is sick, but they don't feel that they are suddenly her ill-equipped parents.

In the dysfunctional family, roles are more rigidly defined, and they are subject to change without notice. Sons or daughters who are taking care of a sick mother may also be expected to be parents to their siblings. The sick mother asks, "Why aren't you looking after your brothers and sisters?" But when the father gets home, he may want his daughter or son to be a child again, so he asks, "Where did my little girl (or little boy) go?"

It is as if there were boxes labeled "bad girl," "good boy," "slave," "best friend," and so on. Parents put the child into a box that is supposed to define his or her behavior, and the child can't get out of the box on his or her own. When the parent is ready, the child will be plucked from one box and placed in the next.

These children learn to look outside themselves to figure out who they are supposed to be on any particular day, and they feel that they are at the mercy of their parents' whims.

As actors, we are required to assume many roles, both in auditions and in the parts we play, but those roles need to be of our own choosing. We need to have a clear, well-defined sense of who we are in order to live with the role changes required by our profession. If we have grown up in a dysfunctional family, establishing this strong sense of self will take some work. This work is described in Part Two, "Tools for Overcoming the Blocks."

Asking for What We Want Versus Accepting What Is Available

In healthy families, children express the emotions they actually feel, rather than the emotions they think they are expected to feel. They learn early on that if they make their needs known, they will usually get fed, diapered, held, played with, or whatever they want, within reason. They learn that they have some degree of control over their world and that the way to get what they want is to ask for it.

As they grow up, they find that all the family members are encouraged to express their needs, points of view, likes, and dislikes. There is a constant exchange of emotional information.

A child from this kind of home visited me recently and said, "I want that carved alabaster beetle on your table." When I told him that it was mine and that I valued it, he asked, "Do you know where I could get one? I really like it." It didn't occur to him that he couldn't have one; it was just a matter of finding out how to go about getting it.

Children in dysfunctional families learn early on that they have only a limited menu of responses from which to choose and that this menu is determined by the adults. They figure out quickly what is available to them in life and ask only for those things — no matter what they actually want. They learn to be satisfied with what is available, and they grow up with almost no idea of what they really feel or really want. Even if they do know what they want, they rarely know how to go about getting it. With the child of a dysfunctional family, the conversation about the alabaster beetle might go like this:

"May I have that carved alabaster beetle?"

"No, that is very valuable to me."

"Oh, I'm sorry. I shouldn't have asked. I'm sorry."

The child would feel that he had made a terrible mistake and would be ashamed of his serious error in judgment.

One of the things we need as actors is a wide range of human experience. If we have been raised in a dysfunctional home, we will need to stretch our minds and hearts considerably to take in experiences that we weren't encouraged to have in our family of origin.

We will need to practice asking ourselves what we feel and what we want and to practice giving ourselves permission to have those things. If we want to play a certain role, we need to tell someone and perhaps fight the subconscious feeling that we will be punished if we ask for something that is not available.

The challenge is to take charge of our own agenda and ask ourselves what we want, not what we think we can have.

The Habit of Telling Lies

We're all human, and no one is entirely faithful to the truth all the time, but in the healthy family people don't usually go out of their way to tell lies. In the dysfunctional family, there is almost nothing to be gained by telling the truth, and lying becomes a way of life.

The children of an alcoholic parent have heard over and over again the lies about why the alcoholic can't go to work, the promises made and broken, the cover-ups presented to the outside world. Lying often seems to make things more comfortable, while telling the truth creates even greater chaos and confusion because it violates the fragile peace constructed from agreed-on lies.

Acting requires telling our deepest truths. This is a whole new world for people who have grown up in dysfunctional families. Clients tell me that they lie in interviews for no compelling reason and then can't remember which lie they have told to whom — or why. They are caught in a giant web of deception and want to break free, but they don't know how.

The entertainment industry is a small world in terms of the people who do the actual hiring, and those people talk to one another. It pays to be truthful, and sometimes it pays to go back and undo some of the damage that's been done — to tell agents and casting directors that we've made some mistakes in the past and how we intend to handle those situations in the future.

Of course, simply becoming aware of the habit of telling lies is not going to solve the problem, but it is the first step. It takes time and the constant reminder that truth is the foundation of our work as actors. The reasons we felt we had to lie as children no longer govern our adult life; now the child in us who learned to lie needs to learn about the safety in truth.

A tool that really works as a reminder and enables us to review when we lie and what we lie about is the placing of notes in a box. Take a shoe box, make a slit in the top, and put it in a convenient place with paper and a pencil beside it. Whenever you lie, make a note of it and place the note in the box. If you are away from home, write the note and place it in the box when you return. Choose a time every week or so (later it can be every month or so), find a comfortable place, and, encircling yourself with kindness, read the notes. Some of them you will be able to laugh at, perhaps some will make you really angry. No matter how they make you feel, try to imagine what the difference in each situation would have been if you had told the truth. You will find that many situations would have worked out better. When you have finished, either burn the notes or put them in a bag and ceremoniously place them in the garbage. The box is empty, you have begun to see what the lies are, and the box will not fill up as quickly again.

This tool can also be used in other situations; you can make notes about times you smiled even though you were angry, times you did not ask for what you wanted, times you were unnecessarily hard on yourself, or times you were late. The irritation of having to stop and write the note is enough to stop some of these unproductive behaviors. The box can also be used between two people to review issues in a safe and supportive environment at a time when discussion is possible.

Lack of Support and the Fear of Taking Risks

In healthy families, people share certain basic assumptions about what their individual relationships are and what it means to be a member of the family. They have common bonds and a certain level of mutual support. They know that, to some extent, they will stand by one another no matter how different their individual directions and tastes.

The opposite is true in dysfunctional families. It is more likely that family members will betray one another than that they will support one another. Their interpretations of their relationships, and of what being a family means, vary widely.

For actors, such a background translates into a fear that the director, teacher, or agent will not understand us and will ridicule or sabotage anything individual or idiosyncratic in our work. Rather than risk this kind of rejection, we try to second-guess what agents and casting directors want, paralyzing our ability to take creative risks and thus often turning in "safe" and less interesting performances. By good luck, magic, serendipity, or brilliance, we have embraced a profession that requires that we become enchanted with taking risks in our work. It is entirely possible to learn how to do that, and we will explore some ways to feel safe about taking risks later in this book.

Individuated Versus Fused Family Members

Healthy families encourage the differences that distinguish their members one from the other. In such families, it is easy to express divergent points of view, to argue about them, and to be honored for being the "different" one. The role of each family member is not defined by the dictates of another member, although all the members are mutually supportive.

In a dysfunctional family, the members are like bags of oil being dropped into a square box, reshaping themselves to fit in with each other. Each must conform to the boundaries or limits set by all the others, and none can make any effort to define its own shape. Any bag that does not conform will be rejected. Similarly, each child in a dysfunctional family has to forge his or her own alliance with the controlling, addicted, or abusive family member. Children may merge so completely that they never form a separate self; they simply fuse and become an appendage.

In a healthy family, children remain separate individuals with their own personalities, interests, and lives. They may do yard work, dishes, and other chores, but the purpose of this work is to support the family as a whole, not to please one specific member whose approval they must win in order to survive. These children love their parents, but they do not merge with them.

People in intimate relationships need clear boundaries, whether the relationships are romantic or creative. We have to know that we are separate from and independent of one another but that we can come together to create something that is beyond our individual capabilities.

Healthy families encourage the formation of these boundaries and teach their children to set them when they move away from the family and out into the world. Dysfunctional families do everything they can to tear down boundaries so that everyone must merge with the controlling person and remain fused forever.

When we are working on a film or are in rehearsal for a play, we must maintain our uniqueness in the face of other actors, the director, and others on the set. If we do not, our performance will start to look like everyone else's. Or we may become the director's pet or slave, rather than a brilliant, idea-generating individual taking a role to levels that the director may never have imagined—but for which he or she will be profoundly grateful.

The Pressure to Grow Up Too Quickly

Healthy families allow children to grow up gradually, with each level of accomplishment and understanding building on the last. These children have time to relax, to explore their world, and to find out about themselves.

In the chaos of a dysfunctional environment, children grow up too quickly under the pressure of multiple responsibilities and stresses. Six-year-olds often have to behave like adults—frightened, confused adults, but adults nevertheless. Life is serious; they don't have time to play, to mature, to experiment.

Playfulness is an important part of creativity, and people who have grown up in dysfunctional families frequently have to learn how to play when they are adults. The child we will discover through the exercises in this book will play an invaluable role in this part of our journey.

The Impact of Shame on the Dream of Success

Shame is a devastating emotion that can distort our concept of who we are. In the lives of actors who grow up in dysfunctional families, shame is an intimate companion; the child feels shame about whatever the family is hiding and about the hiding itself. For those who grow up in healthy families, shame is scarcely an issue; when a parent tells the same story over and over again, or insists on guests eating more than they want, the rest of the family feels mostly just a loving tolerance. The child in such a family might want the parent to stop, but he or she does not have a deep feeling of shame, and is not terrified to ask the parent to stop for fear of being beaten. The feeling is more like, "That's my dad, that's just the way he is."

For actors, shame as a constant companion can have deep consequences, endangering our dream of success. All of us have a dream that we polish and nurture in private. Perhaps we dream of seeing our name in lights, or of playing a particular role, or of making a difference with our work. That dream gives us direction and impetus; it's what started us along the path.

If we come from a dysfunctional family, however, we are used to feeling shame about things that are hidden. So when someone asks, "What is your dream?" we feel ashamed of our private vision. When we bring the dream out into the open, we feel just as we used to feel when we wanted to bring friends home from school but were afraid and ashamed of what they might see there.

When an actor goes to an audition, the director is hoping to see the most intimate parts of his or her soul. If what comes up is shame, that actor is not going to get a lot of work. To be able to bring the dream into the open with honor and pride, we need to work quite consciously with the child part of us, a technique we will discuss in the next chapter.

Creativity and Healing

Through my conversations with actors, I've become convinced that we are driven by three powerful forces:

- The need to reconnect with our creative center.
- The need to be seen and heard for who we truly are (a need that was probably not fulfilled in childhood).
- The need to be healed.

These three forces are so closely connected that they are almost one and the same. In *The Shifting Point,* Peter Brook writes, "Acting is not a way of life, it is a way to life." We need to heal ourselves in order to pursue our work, and we need to pursue our work in order to heal ourselves.

Healing happens when we understand and accept reality, when we can look at events in the past, see them for what they were, and recognize that we are no longer stuck in those circumstances. We no longer need to be afraid of the things that seemed so frightening when we were young—things like a parent's disapproval or the laughter of other children. The work we must do today is to understand what happened in the past so that we are free both to shape our present and our future and to follow our dream.

part two

Tools for Overcoming the Blocks

Genius is nothing more, nor less, than childhood recovered at will.
Charles Baudelaire, *The Painter of Modern Life*

chapter 3
Bringing the Child
into the Present

When I ask actors in consulting sessions, "How old is the kid in you?" I get instant responses. "Five!" "Six!" "Three!" They don't even need to think about it; they just know.

I've asked nonactors this same question, and, although a few answer readily, many come up with more linear, left-brain answers: "You want to know my age?" "I don't have a child, I'm not even married." "Is there a right answer?"

Maybe as actors we are more willing to let our intuition guide us. Maybe our craft teaches us to take emotional risks. Whatever the explanation, this question, "How old is the kid in you?" has proved to be the quickest and most direct route to the traumatic events we need to heal. As we explore what happened at that point in our lives, we almost always discover what made us shut down.

Bringing that lost child into the present to share our creative life is a simple but magical process. It's not difficult or complex, but it does require some openness and a sense of wonder.

We meet a new person when we go back to rescue the child we left behind, and we need to work on our relationship with that person as we would on any new relationship. There are bound to be some rough spots, and it's a good idea not to put off that first, sometimes awkward encounter until the hour before we open in

Othello. Healing the past will give us the strength to be vulnerable, the ability to go to our deepest feelings without losing our sense of self or our mastery of our craft.

Why We Need That Kid

When we left our child behind, we lost some of our freedom. Consciously or unconsciously, we began to edit ourselves. We couldn't concentrate on what we *wanted* to say or do; we were too busy making sure that we didn't say or do anything that would cause trouble. To be ourselves and to express ourselves fully again, we need to make it safe for the child in us to come back.

The adult we have become is now in charge of that child's safety and security. There will be much to teach and much to learn. We will need not only to love and protect our fearful child but also to discipline our rebellious kid.

Finding Our Child

There are five basic things we need to ask or say to our child. The first two are questions, and they are what bring the child back to us. Answer them now. Don't think about the responses. Just say the first thing that comes to mind.

1. *How old is the kid in you?*

Most actors can just let this number pop up. They don't know *why* the kid in them is that age, but they do know how old he or she feels.

2. *What was happening when you were that age?*

This question helps uncover the events that made us sever the connection with our feelings and our creative center. With a little probing, we can usually find the moment or moments of decision.

Often, people remember a happy, golden time just before the trauma began. If happy memories are what come up, we need to ask, "What happened next?" If we keep asking that question, we will come to a time that was very uncomfortable, a time we don't want to think or talk about, a time that makes us quite uneasy.

When we reach that point, when we want to stop doing this exercise and go watch television, we've probably found the moment.

When I asked my client Elaine, an actress in New York, how old the kid in her was, she responded immediately, "Four!" I asked her what had happened when she was four, and she said, "Oh, it was wonderful. I had all my dolls around me, and I took walks in the woods and felt really loved." Nothing uncomfortable there. We explored that whole year of her life and didn't find any negatives—just a happy, carefree child who was the focus of her parents' attention and who seemed to have everything she wanted. But this free, joyous, unencumbered, and unself-conscious spirit was missing from Elaine's acting. Where had it gone?

I kept asking, "What happened next?" Finally I saw Elaine's face change into that of a lonely, unhappy child. All the vitality left her, the very shape of her changed, and she became smaller and completely nonassertive. It was like looking at a different person.

"Oh, yeah, then my little brother was born," she said. That had been the end of her parents' undivided attention, and it had been so traumatic that she began to have severe psychological and behavioral problems. "That year was really awful," she said. "The whole world turned upside down." At school, she had to conform to everybody else's schedules and activities, and when she was at home her place had been taken by the baby. The happy little girl had gone away, to be replaced by a sullen, defensive child whom Elaine had brought with her into adulthood.

In that year, Elaine had lost her child, her internal peace, and her home—both metaphorically and, to her five-year-old mind, literally. It was important for her to validate the pain she felt at her loss. And it was just as important for her to recognize that she could recover her child, her peace, and her home. This idea is often a revelation. We don't dare dream that we could again experience all the joy, spontaneity, and unself-conscious creativity of childhood—but the realization that we *can* starts us on our journey back.

After we've discovered who our child is and where he or she is in time, we can go on to the third step.

3. *Apologize to the child for leaving him or her behind.*

We didn't abandon our child on purpose, but he or she is still hurt and frightened. We need to reassure him or her as we would any child who is hurt and afraid. That child is also probably very angry. In order for the child to let go of the anger, to open up, to be vulnerable, and to love, we need to apologize.

We all find our own way of doing this, but the basic message we need to convey is something like this: "I'm sorry I abandoned you, but in order to survive the circumstances [and here we can mention specifically what was happening], I had to grow up very quickly and I left you back there. I apologize for that."

Some of us are used to this kind of "talking to ourselves," but for others it may not be a comfortable thing to do. Think of it as improvisation, with your own gut feelings providing the voice of the child within. Sometimes my clients talk aloud to their child; sometimes their conversations are silent. Some write their conversations out in script form and then read them over. We may try to talk to our child while walking or running, driving a car or doing the dishes.

The responses that we get as we begin these conversations will vary, too. The child may be delighted to be rediscovered and may tell us right away what's going on and what he or she wants. Or that child may be shy and require some patience and cajoling. The important thing is to put aside whatever embarrassment we might feel in talking to the child and just do it.

We will need to listen closely to what the child has to say so that we know how to respond. We may have to be flexible, perhaps experimenting with a variety of ways of talking with our child in order to find the one that works best for both of us. However these talks evolve, the things we want to provide are love, understanding, acceptance, forgiveness, encouragement, comfort, and trust. It is through this kind of understanding and acceptance, this embracing of the child in all the hurt and all the brilliance, that healing takes place.

4. Ask the child how he or she felt back then.

This step gives the child a chance to talk about the hurt, the pain, the fear, and the anger — and thereby to release them.

When we've had serious estrangements from friends, we don't expect it to be all over and back to normal after a few words of apology. We need to talk about what happened, to tell one another how we felt. There may be anger or tears. For the event to be complete, we need to go back and see it through the other person's eyes.

This is what we do for the child within when we ask how he or she felt. It gives the child a chance to say aloud how scary, or humiliating, or infuriating those events were. He or she has to do that before we can go forward.

The hurt, frightened child needs to be enveloped in unconditional love and support, to know that we will protect him or her from harm, to understand that he or she can begin to relax, to play, to enjoy life, and to trust his or her instincts again. We need to remind our child that the trauma was in the past, that we are here now as protectors, confidants, and nurturers.

Elaine, the actress whose life fell apart when her baby brother was born, apologized to her child and listened to how that child had felt. Afterward, she said, "I'm sorry all that happened. It felt awful, didn't it? But I'm going to make it up to you. I'm going to look after you, see that you're safe and that you have fun. I'm going to make sure you never forget that I love you."

After she said this, Elaine turned to me and asked, "That's what I need now, isn't it? That's exactly why I came here, to find out what was missing, why I feel so empty a lot of the time. I've been hunting everywhere, spending money, doing dumb things, drinking too much . . . and I had it right here all the time. Amazing. Simple, huh?"

Elaine very quickly reclaimed much of the child in her. Her appearance changed so much that friends asked her if she had lost weight, had cut her hair, or was in love. To the last question, she answered yes.

5. *Ask the child what he or she wants now.*

We need to reassure the child within us that now we will be the good, loving parent the child always wanted and that we will listen to what he or she needs. The child may not know what those needs and desires are at first. Like good parents, we must be patient and keep trying.

Similarly, when we're stuck about what to do or which direction to take, it sometimes helps to ask our child. His or her answers are often close to the heart of our true desires. We might let him or her help with these kinds of issues:

- Do we want to take two weeks off this summer and attend an acting workshop in another state?
- Is now the time to move to New York, or is that something we ever really want to do?
- Is that role really right for us, or would it be better to sit this play out and wait for something else?

The child we are seeking can help us find these answers, but we must be careful to notice which facet of the child is speaking to us. We're not looking for the rebellious teenager who is acting out and getting into trouble. His or her anger is just covering the hurt of childhood.

We can't always just go with our child's whims. The child needs healing, love, acceptance, and ways to express his or her imaginative self, but he or she may also need some guidance and gentle discipline, especially at first.

For instance, if the child in us wants to spend a great deal of money on ballet classes or to take a year off to study, we must acknowledge this desire, but we must also let the adult in us have a say. Is it possible? Partly possible? Under what conditions? Where are the funds, and can they be paid back? Do we, the adults, feel comfortable with the risk?

Usually the child within will be happy to go along with any decision that helps us get on with "our work." But if the child responds by sulking and pouting, we need to remember that that is how children are sometimes (although usually not for long).

Sometimes being a loving parent means drawing lines and saying no. Gradually the discipline and loving that were not available earlier in life become comfortable and welcome to the child.

As we grow closer to our child, and as some of the old hurt and anger dissipate, he or she will begin to help us make choices that truly serve us and our work. The child we find through this process is the one who simply *knows* the answers and *knows* that he or she will act. There is no question about it, no thought about whether he or she will do it well or about what people will think. This child doesn't *think* about acting; it simply flows forth naturally, effortlessly, and spontaneously.

Magic touches everything this child does. This is the child who returns again and again to the creative well and comes back bearing treasures.

Parenting the Child Within: Case Studies

Working with the child requires creativity and courage, and we may need professional support. Many of my clients have gone into individual therapy or have gotten involved with ACA or other groups. As the following case studies show, there are many ways to bring the child into the present in order to break through our blocks.

Sharon: Getting past the open door

Sharon is a comedian who lives and works in Los Angeles and has done well in film. She came to see me because she was becoming increasingly uncomfortable in interviews. She felt almost paralyzed, especially at the moment when she actually walked through a casting director's door.

This seemed strange for someone with her credits and experience, but she said she'd always been uncomfortable in this situation. She had told herself that her discomfort would go away, but instead it seemed to be getting worse.

After we had talked about what her discomfort felt like, I asked Sharon, "How old is the kid in you?" Her immediate response was "Five!"

Sharon is a small, feisty woman. When she was five, she actually looked closer to three and a half. She was the youngest in a large family, and her function was to be the family clown. She made everyone laugh, and they all adored her.

All the children attended a one-room schoolhouse in Nebraska, and joining all her friends and siblings at school was a big event in Sharon's life. When the day finally arrived, she set off alone, as she had wanted, with her lunch and her new school supplies. But when she got to the school and walked up the steps, Sharon found that she was too small to reach the door handle. She tried and tried, but it was no use.

She actually left the school and tried to invent something to do to pass the day, but she realized that her brothers and sisters would tell her parents, so she went back.

As she stretched high above her head for one last try at the handle, the door flew open. Standing beside the open door was the teacher and, behind him, the other children. They were all laughing. This was the first time that Sharon had ever been embarrassed by laughter. She felt this embarrassment again when the older kids told the story at dinner that night and everyone laughed.

At that moment the clown part of Sharon went into an eclipse that lasted a long time. Now, as an adult, she felt the eclipse beginning to return. She felt as if she were walking a tightrope between comedy and humiliation. It was exhausting, and it made her very anxious.

When we uncovered this incident, Sharon exclaimed, "Of course, that's it! The feelings are exactly the same!" The instant she realized how the feelings of panic and humiliation had gotten tied together, they largely disappeared. There was still work to be done, of course, and Sharon spent a good deal of time getting to know her child, talking with her about how she had felt back then, and reassuring her.

Before she goes to see casting directors now, Sharon spends a little extra time with the child in her, reminding her that she no longer needs to feel panicked or ashamed, and her problem has all but disappeared.

Joe: Relinquishing anger

Joe is a twenty-seven-year-old actor who has enjoyed considerable success in television commercials, motion pictures, and
guest appearances on television series. He is very attractive in a
clean-cut, preppie way — tall and blue-eyed, with dark hair and a
crinkly smile that lights up his face. But just beneath the surface,
sadness lurks. In unguarded moments, he sometimes looks like
a hurt little boy.

Joe came to see me because he was getting married and his
fiancée, Janet, was concerned about the anger she saw in him. He
was always angry — at his agent, at casting directors, other actors,
directors, producers, and almost everyone in a position of power
in the industry. Janet was afraid that some of this rage would
bleed through into their marriage, and she never got a satisfactory
answer when she asked, "Why do you act if it makes you so
angry?"

It was a good question, one that Joe and I began to explore. He
was particularly defensive and antagonistic with his agent, Len.
We talked about why he was so defensive with anyone in power
and why he kept repeating the pattern of setting himself up to be
rejected, then getting angry at the agent and saying, in essence,
"Get lost, I didn't want it anyway."

"How old is the kid in you?" I asked.

"Five!" he replied immediately, and then looked surprised
that he had been so certain.

"What happened when you were five?"

The story came pouring out. When Joe was five, his natural
father had died and the "golden time" in his life ended. His
mother, left with nothing, started to drink heavily. She had a
series of affairs with men who were usually alcoholic and abusive, both to her and to Joe and his older brothers.

When Joe was eleven, his mother married one of these men,
and the situation grew even worse. Joe remembers being locked
in his room, listening to his mother being beaten. He was afraid
to go to sleep and afraid to stay awake and hear her screams.

He felt very angry — with his mother, with his father for dying, with his stepfather, and with the kids at school who seemed to have easy, pleasant, secure lives with none of the trauma that he experienced at home. As he grew older, these "preppies" became the particular target of his rage, and he began acting out with them, getting into fights at school and causing more and more trouble. He drove fast cars and motorcycles, and his wild activities led to trouble with the police. He was even thrown in jail a few times.

As we talked, Joe began to see that, because he had never dealt with his anger toward his father, mother, stepfather, and others in authority, he had transferred that anger to people with power in the industry, and especially to his agent.

He would get into screaming fights with Len and crash out of his office, but he stayed with Len as his agent so that he could continue to play out the transference. He had to have someone on whom to put his anger, and it had to be someone who looked as though he had control over Joe's life. The fact that Joe was now disguised as one of the preppies he hated made no difference; inside he was that tough, rebellious, motorcycle-riding "hood" he had been at sixteen.

All the energy Joe could have been putting into his work was going into the anger. In a way, the anger took the place of his work. It was amazing that Joe had been as successful as he had been, given this handicap, but it was also clear that he could accomplish much more if he dissolved some blocks and freed all that energy.

Again, we went back to the child. Anger is almost always a mask for hurt, and the child Joe had been at five when his father died and his world fell apart was still trying to cover up the hurt with a veneer of rage. Joe needed to begin a relationship with that child, as well as with the rebellious teenager.

The first thing he did was to apologize to little Joey. Joe remembered the time around his father's death as he spoke to the little boy he had left behind.

JOE: I'm sorry I left you back then, but it was the only way I knew how to survive. Things were so bad and it hurt so much. I grew up real fast, and you were left there with all that pain . . . I'm sorry.

Joey is sulky and won't look up. He wants to trust, but he's afraid.

JOEY: Thanks, but it still hurts — a lot.

Joe knows this hurt. The child in him has felt it every day.

JOE: I know. Me too. But now we have a chance to do what we've always dreamed of doing. I'm an actor now. Do you want to act?

An eager face looks up.

JOEY: You mean it?

JOE: Yeah, I do. And I need you. I'm making you a promise that I'll never let you get hurt again. You can trust me now. I'm not going to butt out on you.

Joe's tears were both for himself and for the little boy he had been. He had to let that child shed the tears of hurt that he had never shed, and to reassure his little boy that everything was all right now, that the adult Joe would take care of him.

Joe actually worked with two children: the hurt five-year-old and the rebellious sixteen-year-old. He talked with both of them regularly and eventually began to let the two younger Joeys become part of him.

When Len called and asked Joe to stop by so that they could talk about a minor but ongoing role in a popular television series, Joe figured he'd better get on the same team with the kids because he didn't want to blow this opportunity. He set aside some time when he could be alone, and had these conversations.

JOE: So, how do you feel about this meeting with Len?

JOEY AT SIXTEEN: The guy's a jerk. He's never done anything for me, and he never will.

JOE: What about that insurance commercial, and the guest shots on the soap?

JOEY AT SIXTEEN: Yeah, well, he did those for himself. I don't know what he has against me, but he acts like he's better than I am, like he's doing me some big favor. He's got it easy, sitting behind that desk. Let *him* go on these auditions. I don't need the aggravation.

JOE: Hey, what's really wrong? How come you have that chip on your shoulder?

JOEY AT SIXTEEN: I don't have a chip on my shoulder.

JOE: Yeah, you do. You always get upset before you see Len, and you always blame him if you don't get a part. Nothing the guy does is right for you. Why does Len make you so angry?

JOEY AT SIXTEEN: I just want to punch him out every time I see him.

JOE: Why?

JOEY AT SIXTEEN: I don't know, he's got me on a string. He's got all the cards, and I don't like it. He's got all the power. I can't do anything without him, and he's trying to keep me down.

JOE: Do you think getting angry with him helps?

JOEY AT SIXTEEN: Probably not, but I don't know what else to do.

JOE: What do you really feel when you're with Len?

JOEY AT SIXTEEN: Small. Weak. Powerless. Frustrated. Sometimes I feel like I want to cry, so I scream at him instead.

JOE: Yeah, I know. Does he remind you of anyone?

JOEY AT SIXTEEN: My stepfather. There was nothing any of us could do about him. I got so mad because I was scared, but I couldn't go after him or he'd get worse, so I took it out on cars and drinking and all those crazy things.

JOE: And on Len?

JOEY AT SIXTEEN: I guess. Not too smart, huh?

JOE: Well, you just did what you felt you had to do, and you didn't really know what was going on. Our stepfather was awful; it's okay to be angry at him. But it's not doing much good to be mad at Len, is it?

JOEY AT SIXTEEN: No, I guess not. But when I'm not angry, I'm sad. I don't think I can take being that sad.

JOE: Yeah, I know what you mean. I feel like that, too. We have a lot to be sad about, but not at interviews, and not around

Len, because then you get angry. Our stepfather was mean, and you're right to be angry with him. But don't get him confused with Len, just because Len has authority. Let me handle Len. I don't like him a lot, but he's a good agent. Betcha we can turn this around.

Joe got his teenager to talk about what was really troubling him, validated his feelings, and let him know that he would take care of him. As they continued to talk, the younger Joe opened up more and more, learned to trust both himself and the adult Joe, and ultimately let go of the destructive side of his anger.

Before Joe met with Len, he also sat down with the five-year-old Joey.

JOE: How are you doing in there, Joey?

JOEY AT FIVE: Not so good. I'm scared. I don't want to be hurt again.

JOE: I know how you feel. But I don't think Len is going to hurt us. If we don't get the part, it's not because he didn't want us to or because he doesn't like us.

JOEY AT FIVE: No?

JOE: Nah. So what really hurts?

JOEY AT FIVE: When Dad died. And the other man came.

JOE: I know. Me too. But that happened a long time ago, and we have each other now. I won't ever let anything happen like what happened with the other man. That's over. I'm not going to let you get hurt again. So how do you feel about going to see Len on Thursday?

JOEY AT FIVE: I get scared of him. When things don't go right or I don't get parts, I feel like I did when Dad died and everything crashed in.

JOE: I know. But Joey, it's different now. Len isn't Dad, or Mom, or the other man. Len's really on our side.

JOEY AT FIVE: He is?

JOE: Sure he is. Do you think we could give him a little more of a chance to prove it? You can let me know whenever you get uncomfortable.

JOEY AT FIVE: Okay, maybe I could do that.

JOE: What do you want to do afterward for a reward?
JOEY AT FIVE: A movie and popcorn . . . lots of butter!

The young Joey's presence has given Joe an intuitive, playful quality that his work never had before. Getting to know Joey has also helped Joe find ways of rewarding himself that are supportive rather than destructive. Instead of getting drunk or staying out late as the sixteen-year-old Joey might have done, he has worked with both younger Joeys and imposed a gentle discipline so that they are more likely to choose nondestructive rewards — like a movie and popcorn.

Through his relationships with the two younger Joeys, Joe has begun to see himself more clearly and to understand the ways he has been sabotaging himself both personally and professionally. As he went back and let himself experience the hurt, working through it with the help of Janet and a therapist whom he saw once a week, his anger became much more manageable. His relationship with Len has improved, and eliminating some of this tension has resulted in more work. Best of all, Joe is no longer living and working in reaction to his past.

Beth: Regaining a lost childhood

Some people find it very difficult at first to remember things that happened when they were children. If we can't recall much about our childhood, there's probably a reason we are blocking it. When these memories just won't come, a therapist or support group can sometimes help.

Many of my clients can recall only a few pictures from their childhoods. With consistent work, we can build up a sense of what happened from these random fragments. There are always little threads and strands, details that lead us back. Perhaps a photograph, glimpses of a picnic, or the time we played the third flower in the second row in a school play will open the door. When we relax, something usually surfaces. It helps to think about the fragments we do have, let ourselves feel the emotions that surround them, or even write about them. Gradually, more details will surface.

Beth is thirty-six, lives in California, and came to me because "I can't get beyond a certain point as an actress. My teacher keeps telling me to relax and have fun. I understand that in my head, but I can't let go and do it. I'm not sure I know what fun is."

Beth could remember the chores and responsibilities of her childhood clearly, but she could not recall playing. As the fourth of seven children, she felt as if she had had five parents and three children. Beth had been given almost total responsibility for the three younger kids, and she felt as if she had been a mother for as long as she could remember.

The older kids wouldn't play with her or allow her to join in anything they did because "You're too small . . . You'll spoil the fun . . . You'll be in the way . . . You can't walk fast enough." She always felt inadequate, yet at the same time she was expected to look after the babies and the toddler. She had to feed them, bathe them, do their laundry, take them for walks, and put them to bed.

She has only the faintest memories of childhood aside from this caretaking role, but she is very good at mothering and feels secure as a mother in her adult life.

"How old is the kid in you?" I asked.

She responded, "I don't know who that person is."

"Do you have children?"

"Oh, yes! My wonderful daughter Peggy is eight."

We started talking about Peggy, and Beth said, "She's so wonderful. She plays and she laughs . . . That's what you're talking about, isn't it?"

"Do you play with Peggy?" I asked.

"No, I don't know how to play."

The first assignment I gave Beth was to start playing with Peggy, to set up a tea party under the dining room table, to switch chairs with Peggy at dinner, to do whatever silly thing struck her fancy. I told her, "Now you have two children. You have Peggy and you have yourself at that age, and you need to pay attention to both of them."

This wasn't easy at first; Beth had to learn how to play from her daughter. Gradually she started to remember things about her own childhood. Beth has shed many tears for the child who missed out on so much and who spent her younger years on a treadmill. That child would come home from school, cook dinner, take care of the kids, do the laundry, clean up, pack lunches for the next day, do her homework, and go to bed so she could get up in the morning and go to school.

The more Beth remembers, the more free she becomes and the more accessible her child is to her. She is discovering how imaginative, playful, and funny she can be, and is constantly surprising herself. Her acting is beginning to have truth in it, and she is learning to operate from her feelings about a scene or a character. She tells me that her husband and Peggy are having much more fun with her.

Beth is also beginning to free herself from the notion that her only role in life is to care for people. She used to have trouble believing that there were film or stage roles for her, that there were agents who wanted to work with her, that she had a right to be in a casting director's office without taking care of him or her.

Beth is beginning to realize that people may actually be interested in her talent, and that she doesn't have to look after the crew or cook everyone's meals to belong on a set. She is learning to use that caretaking energy to take care of *herself*.

James: Understanding the cut-and-run kid

James was born when his parents were over forty. He had an older sister who was twenty-one, and he was raised essentially as an only child. His father, Arthur, was an alcoholic who came home from his butcher shop tired and irritable at the end of each day and who often abused James both physically and psychologically.

Occasionally, on a whim or when he was "maintaining" his alcoholism, Arthur was warm and affectionate, but more often he was impatient and intolerant. James could never understand what it was that produced the good reactions, and he never knew what to expect.

At four, all this creative child wanted was to be loved, approved of, and appreciated for himself. He was highly imaginative, and has vivid memories of the kinds of scenes that occurred when Arthur came home at night. James would eagerly rush toward his father.

JAMES: Daddy, Daddy! I was a green leaf on a tall, tall tree, and there was a big wind, and I blew all the way to China.

James would cling to his father's legs while Arthur tried to get him off.

ARTHUR: That's nonsense and you know it. I don't want to hear that kind of shit from you. Why can't you behave like a normal kid? Why can't I have a normal kid?

Arthur would then pick James up, stride into the house, open the door to James's room, throw him inside, and slam the door.

ARTHUR: You stay there until you figure out how to behave. [Shouting to his wife.] Mary! Mary! I don't know what you do to that kid; he's telling those lies again. I want a normal kid . . . Mary! *Mary!*

All James wanted was Arthur's approval, but when he tried to share a special secret with his father he got hurt mentally and physically. He was alone, confused, and guilty because his father was screaming at his mother. He thought that if he could just figure out how to do things *right,* then everything would be better. So the next night he would try a different approach. When his father came home, he would do nothing. He even thought about hiding, but his father got home before he could decide where.

ARTHUR: What's the matter? Cat got your tongue?

James would remain silent and still, trying to protect himself, wishing he were invisible.

ARTHUR: I'll teach you to show me some respect. I'll teach you not to answer me!

Once again, Arthur would grab James under one arm, stride into the house, open the door to James's room, and throw him inside. After the door slammed, James would hear his father's voice shouting.

ARTHUR: Mary! Mary! That kid's gotta learn some respect. He's not going to get any dinner. Mary! It's your fault. You're too soft on him. You encourage him.

It's hard for children to understand that they don't cause the circumstances around them, that they are simply part of a flawed system. Sometimes it takes a long time to understand that not all systems operate in this flawed way.

When James grew up, he became a successful comedian whose specialty was black humor. But he had some problems that he knew were rooted in these early experiences. If he walked into the office of someone with authority — an agent, a casting director, a producer — and that person was arguing with someone on the phone, James somehow felt that the disagreement was his fault. He had brought the childhood guilt about his father's actions into his adult professional life.

Logic told him that he wasn't to blame. He knew that in the entertainment industry, argument is often part of negotiating and exchanging information, but he couldn't shake the gut feeling that he was the cause of these angry encounters.

When the person in authority said, "So, tell me something about yourself," James felt that whatever he said would be wrong. He would go through the whole interview feeling guilty. Obviously, he wasn't as effective as he might have been.

Both of these responses — the guilt and the feeling that whatever he did or said would be the wrong thing — were in place by the time James was four. In order to turn them around, he had to go back and find that four-year-old James.

The first step was to realize that none of the chaos at home had been his fault. He had spent a lot of time as a child trying to figure out what he was doing wrong — or what he was doing right on those rare occasions when his father was affectionate with him — and he had carried this habit of second-guessing himself into his adult life. Through his work with Adult Children of Alcoholics, he came to understand the chaotic downward spiral of an alcoholic's life. When he realized that his father's behavior had nothing to do with him, he saw that his father's anger and violence had just been erratic, alcoholic behavior.

There are many different ways to work with the child within, and James's method was different from Joe's or Beth's. Much of his reparenting involved the imagination. His childhood would have been entirely different if his father's homecomings had been more like this:

ARTHUR: So, what did you do today?
JAMES: I was a green leaf on a tall, tall tree, and a big wind came, and I blew all the way to China.
ARTHUR: Well, tell me, what was it like in China?

When I asked James what it would have felt like if his father had responded to him in this way, his face lit up. I could see the child in him clearly. Tears came to his eyes as he said, "I can feel that. I can really feel that. Hey, if I can feel that now, I guess I haven't lost it, have I?" His journey back had begun.

James created many of these healing images and scenes, and had many conversations with his child over a period of time. He apologized to his child for having abandoned him, and explained why this had happened. He listened to how the child had felt at that time. Sometimes they would just talk, and James would listen to the child's fears and hurts, reassuring him that everything was all right now and reminding him that he didn't have to react as he had back then.

They came to know one another well, and James learned to sense quickly when the child in him was feeling uncomfortable and about to shift into old, negative behavior patterns. When his child started feeling as if everything were his fault and he couldn't do anything right, James reminded him that he was no longer in a dysfunctional environment; he could relax and respond to people authentically and confidently.

When one issue has been clarified, understood, and dealt with, another usually surfaces. Soon after James had gotten a handle on the guilt and can't-do-anything-right issues, he began to notice another pattern that was hurting his career.

Whenever things went wrong and he started to feel uncomfortable, James would take off suddenly and go to another city without telling anyone. If he were in Chicago, he would get on a plane and be in Los Angeles that afternoon — without preparing the people in Chicago for the fact that he was leaving or the people in Los Angeles for the fact that he was arriving. The problem might be personal or professional, but his response was always to cut and run.

James was acquiring a reputation for being unreliable. Agents, directors, and producers were furious with him when he pulled this disappearing act, and James couldn't understand why. All he knew was that when things got tough, his instinct was to escape, to isolate himself from everyone. He always thought that things would be different somewhere else.

Even though we had explored much of James's childhood, I asked him again, "How old is the kid in you?"

"Four!"

"What happened when you were four?"

A whole new story began to pour out, one that solved the riddle of the isolation strategies and destructive escapes.

When James was four, his father had been about to lose the butcher shop, and the family was in dire financial straits. His mother, Mary, the co-alcoholic whose main goal in life was to protect her husband from the negative consequences of his drinking, had taken in ten children about James's age and cared for them all day to make ends meet. Until then, the daytime, when his father was at work, had been James's only respite from chaos. It had been the only time when he could breathe easily, when things were calm and peaceful.

Now, with ten preschoolers in his home during the day, he had lost this precious time of peace, quiet, and safety. In addition to one large unpredictable person, he now had to deal with a whole group of smaller unpredictable people. Now everything in his life was chaotic, twenty-four hours a day, and all he wanted to do was isolate himself from the upheaval and unpredictability.

Every morning when the children arrived, James went into his room and locked the door. When I asked him what he did in there, he said quietly, "Played." I decided to press the issue.

What he had done was to take all his toys—stuffed animals, building blocks, trains, cars, and so on—and arrange them in an oblong shape on the floor. Then he would lie down in the middle of them. This was his grave, and all the animals and toys would tell him how much they missed him and how wonderful he was. There were variations on this game, and many types of funeral service, but this is how James had survived emotionally, how he had gotten the tenderness and validation he craved.

The mock funerals marked the beginning of a secret life for James that had kept his creativity alive, but it had isolated him almost completely from other people. He still has difficulty communicating with people and is often misunderstood. Relationships are his biggest challenge. It's little wonder that he leaves town at the first sign of trouble, just as he used to escape to his room. And it's little wonder that his humor is a dark, gallows humor.

James knows that even though his work is very good and he gets cast a lot, his erratic behavior isn't helping his career. At this point, the damage is not so much to his work as to the politics of his work. Producers say, "Yeah, his work is fantastic, but he's a pain to be around." Or "He's unreliable. Try going on location with him for six weeks. You never know if he's going to show up. Who needs that?"

James has had to let the child in him know that he is loved and accepted for who he is, and that he has a right to his own internal peace and place in the world. At the same time, he is working hard in therapy to change his patterns of thought and behavior and to stop running away. But sometimes he catches himself and says sheepishly, "I did it again, didn't I?"

We don't change the emotional habits of a lifetime overnight. We all work at our own speed, and it's a lifelong process. As James is coming to realize, we don't have to get it all done tomorrow.

Susan: Hearing what isn't said

One of Susan's most powerful childhood memories is of her father's booming laugh. He laughed after he said, "You're a pretty little girl." He also laughed after he said, "You're stupid!" She never knew what he meant, but the laughter always made it seem as if he meant the opposite of what he said. Her father was a big man with a voice to match, so both the laughter and the words were overwhelming to her.

The members of Susan's family were extremely unsupportive of one another and continually betrayed one another's secrets and confidences. When Susan heard laughter in another part of the house, she always felt sure that they were talking about her. Her father frequently ridiculed her at the dinner table, and her older siblings always joined in the laughter.

Oddly, or perhaps not so oddly, Susan grew up to be a talented comedian. The fact that laughter tended to send her back into these childhood feelings of insecurity, confusion, and betrayal was a major stumbling block to her career. So was her belief that what people said was the opposite of what they meant, and the fear that someone knew all her secrets and would betray her for no reason at all.

Susan found this combination almost paralyzing. Her brain heard one thing, but her feelings told her that the opposite was being said. In auditions she just wanted to creep away, hoping that no one would notice her. Early in her career, Susan had dreaded going into casting offices because she knew that if she got nervous she would do the opposite of what was asked, crumble under the pressure of feeling exposed, and fall apart if the casting director laughed — which, as a comedian, is what she was trying to achieve.

Her conversations with her child centered around the issue of trust. She had to learn to accept and trust herself just as she was, and to remind little Susie that others were not out to get her, as she believed her family had been. Now, laughter was an acknowledgment of her talent, rather than an indication that people were lying or trying to humiliate her.

Susan had been working with her child for some time, and probably should have had the following conversation *before* a difficult interview with a casting director, but hindsight is twenty-twenty, and sometimes we learn more by making mistakes. Once Susan's child heard the casting director laugh, she wanted out of there. Susan had to work very hard not to give way to the old fears. When she got home, Susan sat down with her child and talked it over.

SUSAN: What happened in there? What was so scary?

SUSIE: They laughed at me. I hate it when people laugh at me.

SUSAN: I know. But they laughed because we were funny. We made them laugh.

SUSIE: It felt like when Dad laughed at me. He'd say, "You're a real pretty little girl," and then he'd laugh that awful loud laugh, and I'd feel stupid.

SUSAN: Honey, the casting director isn't Dad. He wanted us to be funny. I loved it that he laughed; it means we did good work. I remember Dad's laugh — I hated it. But I'm not going to let you get hurt. I'm there all the time; you can trust me now. You know what? You *are* pretty — you're pretty and I love you . . . and I like having you around.

This talk took place a year ago. Susan still has moments of panic, but her conversations with Susie have made a big difference in the way she feels about interviewing and working. In fact, she rarely has to sit down and have specific conversations with Susie at this point. She has merged with Susie in the present, and is able to allow all the wonderful, off-the-wall, childlike parts of Susie to come through safely in her work. She is funnier than ever, and only occasionally does she have a twinge of discomfort when people laugh.

A casting director recently said to her, "This character has to be attractive. You're very attractive and a good comedian. Let's see what you can do." There was a moment when the younger Susie wanted to run out the door, but it was only a moment, and Susan got the job.

Sam: Editing genius

Working with Sam taught me another technique for getting in touch with the child within. Sam, a structural engineer who had done well as an actor, felt that his acting career was not progressing as it should.

When I first saw Sam, he had a number of good credits and was becoming increasingly convinced that he wanted acting to be his major focus. It was what he most wanted to do, yet the larger the roles became, the more uncomfortable he felt. He was aware that there was something wrong, and he knew he had to make changes, but he hadn't the slightest idea how to go about it.

He watched others working and admired their ability to let go and be spontaneous. As much as he envied them, however, he didn't seem to be able to work from his feelings without first evaluating what he thought the result would be. Sam was a brilliant man, but so intellectual and left-brained that he had difficulty imagining how his child would feel about anything. When I asked him how his child felt about the possibility of being a successful full-time actor, he began, "Well, I think that probably I feel . . ." For Sam, even emotions had become ideas that he had to extract from his left brain.

When I asked him other questions designed to elicit feelings, he stared into space. I asked him where he had gone, and he replied, "Oh, I was just trying to figure out whether my child would feel this way or that way." Again, the left brain was hard at work.

I decided to bypass the child altogether for the time being and simply asked Sam to pretend that he was a famous Broadway star. He got into the experience immediately. I could actually see a physical change in him. All of his child's playfulness, spontaneity, excitement, and joy bubbled to the surface, and he stood there as the star/child/adult in all his glory, able to let go of his intellect just long enough to feel the dream for a few seconds.

Sam had been an extremely intelligent and talented youngster. His father was a well-known New York trial attorney whose powerful presence had terrified Sam. The father would say, "My boy is the next Einstein. Move over Einstein, Sam is going to take your place." This not only embarrassed Sam, it set him up to lose. If he did anything less than Einstein had done, he would be a failure.

Sam began to be careful around his parents, to edit any opinions or accomplishments that might prompt this kind of effusive praise. He didn't like being told that he was brilliant, for this made him feel that he had to be perfect. In addition, his father expected each of his performances — academic, musical, or artistic — to be an improvement over the last.

When his father said, "Sammy's the smartest kid I've ever seen — he's a genius," Sam knew it wasn't true. His response was to hide, to conceal himself and his accomplishments from his parents, to avoid making waves. He never showed them his drawings or paintings, and quite deliberately never excelled as a pianist (although that is something he longs to do as an adult) because his father would have said, "See? He's a Paderewski!"

Sam's life became a process of editing and denying an emotional investment in anything. Of course, beneath the facade he cared deeply and was extremely frustrated.

Both personally and professionally, Sam became a master at giving people just enough to satisfy the requirements, but not so much that they would think him brilliant or exceptional in any way. He had chosen structural engineering as a profession largely because it is finite and precise and generally doesn't require much emotional investment. He was a good structural engineer, he was a good actor, but he had trained himself to reveal nothing special in any area.

Sam's solution had isolated him in two ways: from his own creative center, and from other people. He is finding that this isolation no longer works for him as he approaches thirty-five. He wants deeper connections with people, and he wants more from his work. The creative imperative is catching up with him.

Letting go of these carefully structured survival habits takes work. They were built up and reinforced over a period of years and can't be eliminated overnight, but the system can be dismantled and replaced with one that answers Sam's present career needs rather than his old survival needs.

He is beginning to see how the editing process hurts not only his work but also his ability to *get* work. When he edits himself with casting directors, he doesn't get cast, even though he knows they would want him if they saw what he could really do. The editing gives him a certain twisted control because he is in charge of how much people find out about him, and he can feel superior without having to accept much praise. Moreover, he avoids having to make additional editing decisions about how to play the part once he's cast. But it costs him dearly.

The exercise of imagining himself as a Broadway star gave Sam access to his child's energy and enthusiasm, but he still has to work to keep from lapsing back into intellectualism. Because of his iron control, there are really two little boys in Sam: the one with the intuition, feelings, and instinctive wisdom, and the one who is always trying to figure out the right answers and protect himself with his mind. Sam's child often takes an oddly intellectual turn, and when we are working together I often have to tell him, "No, not *that* little boy. The *other* little boy, the playful one."

Sam is getting better at staying in touch with his feelings, and the results can be seen in his personal life as well as in his acting. His responses are more authentic and more richly textured than they were before. His work has a quality of truth. His relationships have improved dramatically.

I have also noticed physical changes. His face used to be a mask; now it's filled with life and reflects his increasingly varied emotions. The tone and color of his skin are more vibrant. He has more energy, and the muscle fatigue and other symptoms that he has experienced for years are disappearing.

Accepting praise has been one of Sam's most difficult issues, but he is learning that the satisfaction of knowing he's doing good work, and of having his work praised by other people, is a much richer experience than the emotional numbness that used to take all his energy. He is becoming willing to let his brilliance show, and is starting to reap the rewards.

Jane: Blocking beauty and pain

Jane is an actress in her early thirties who lives in California. Early in her career Jane had worked a lot, but the larger the roles became the less frequently she was cast. She came to me because she felt that she didn't "belong" as an actress and that there were no roles for her. She also told me that there was something buried in the back of her head that she needed to talk about, but that she was not quite sure what it was.

Jane had been adopted. Her parents had always told her that they had "chosen" her. To Jane, this had implied some kind of performance on her part, but the details of what she had done to make them choose her were never clear. In any case, she had never felt that she could measure up to that initial performance, whatever it had been. Having been put up for adoption had also made her feel that maybe there wasn't really a place for her in this world. As an actress, this translated into the belief that there were no roles for her.

Jane had enormous problems with casting directors and directors. She was always afraid that if she were chosen again, she would be just as confused as she had always been about what was expected of her.

The result was that Jane would do *anything* in order to belong. She waited for other actors to take the lead and made her own actions fit with theirs. She never demanded space or time for her own character. Whenever she made a statement, it sounded like a question or an apology. She merged with anyone who would let her; her work had little strength or momentum of its own.

In addition to feeling as if she didn't belong, Jane had always sensed that she was hiding from something. Her efforts to find out what it could be finally revealed the child within. The child in Jane was several different ages; her shutting down and closing herself off from her feelings had been a gradual process that had taken place over a period of about twelve years.

This happens for all of us to some extent—few of us have only one incident that is solely responsible for our blocks—but the progression of Jane's shutting down had several clear milestones, and each of them had to do with her being beautiful.

Jane remembers that when she was six she would put on little shows, dancing and singing in front of the television. She loved pretty things. One day her mother dressed her up in a pretty new dress and took her to a shopping mall. Everyone commented on what a beautiful little girl she was, and some of the women at the new modeling school made a big fuss over her. Jane and her mother were both thrilled, and told her father about it that evening.

His response was, "Well, she's never going to modeling school. No daughter of mine is ever going to be a model! Models come to no good."

Jane didn't understand her father's response, but her interpretation was that there was something wrong with being pretty, and especially with knowing it. Being aware that you were a pretty little girl was bad, even if some people made a fuss over you.

Five years later, when Jane was eleven, her friend Kate was going to enroll in a modeling school. Kate's mother worked and wasn't able to go with her to register, so Jane and her mother went with Kate instead. Fate took a hand, Kate decided that she didn't want to take the class after all, and Jane's mother agreed to assume the deposit made by Kate's mother. She paid the rest of the tuition and enrolled Jane in the class.

People had been telling Jane for years that she should be a model because she was so pretty. It sounded like fun, but she hadn't actively pursued it out of fear of her father's response. Now, not feeling quite as overwhelmed by her father as she had been at six, Jane was excited by the prospect of modeling school. Her father, however, was incensed.

"No daughter of mine is going to throw her life away," he stated. "I can't pay for every little whim that crosses your mind. I'll either give you this modeling school or I'll pay for college. Which is it going to be? You have to decide now."

Jane was only eleven years old and not in a position to make this kind of decision. She had no idea what college meant, whether she wanted to go, or what she wanted to do with her life. All she knew was that she wanted to be in the modeling class, and that is what she told her father. In bed that night she listened fearfully to her parents' raised voices — but she was going to modeling school.

Jane loved the school and took naturally to modeling. She was beautiful, and she could present herself and the clothes she wore in an artful way that gave her a genuine creative outlet. She felt that she had found her niche in life. As a successful teen model, she was getting paid for her work and being acknowledged by other professionals, and she felt good about herself.

The dark side of Jane's life around that time — and this was the thing she had felt was buried in the back of her head when she first came to see me — was that when she was thirteen her adoptive brother had raped her on four different occasions. She had never mentioned this to anyone before, but now she felt that it might have something to do with her feeling that she did not belong, and she suspected that, in her mind, she had connected these incidents to the fact that she was beautiful.

Jane's looks had seemed to be the source of her troubles, and this feeling was exacerbated when she was fifteen and came close to being raped again by some boys at a high school party. Again she told no one, but she was beginning to accumulate evidence that being beautiful caused both emotional turmoil and actual physical danger.

At the age of fifteen, Jane subconsciously decided that whatever benefits she was enjoying from being pretty — the joy she got from modeling, the money, the sense of expression, accomplishment, and self-esteem — were not worth the pain and danger. After the incident at the party, she started to put on weight. She felt less attractive and therefore safer. Being beautiful was no longer an issue in her life, and boys didn't pursue her.

By the time she graduated from high school and most of her friends had gone off to college, she had gained so much weight that she could no longer continue her modeling career. Her father stuck to the ultimatum he had made when she was eleven and refused to provide money for college.

In addition to being a successful model throughout high school, Jane had played the lead in almost all the high school plays. Her teachers had always encouraged her to think of acting as a career. She had started down this path and things had gone well for a while, but gradually the feelings of not belonging and not wanting to be noticed became almost disabling.

Jane needed to reassure the little girl in her that she was safe, that she belonged, that she was loved unconditionally, that it was all right to be beautiful, that she didn't have to hide or be ashamed of who she was, and that she had a right to whatever means of self-expression she chose. This is part of her first conversation with Jane at age fourteen.

JANE: So, how does it feel back there?

JANE AT FOURTEEN: Awful. I feel ashamed and dirty. You know when my picture would be in the paper as a model and people would think I was perfect? But I knew how bad things really were. I was scared all the time that people would find out how things really were.

JANE: I remember, and I'm sorry I left you like I did. I didn't know any better — but I know better now, and I want you around. I love you and need you, and I'm not going to let you get hurt again. You know, you *are* pretty, and you were a great model. What our brother did was his fault, not our fault, and I'm going to do something about that, so it won't frighten you anymore.

JANE AT FOURTEEN: I feel like I don't belong. I should run away. There isn't any place for me . . . I don't know why they chose me.

It took Jane some time to get all the past talked through, but she stuck with it, and then it became a tool for the present.

JANE AT FOURTEEN: I don't want to go to this audition.

JANE: Why not?

JANE AT FOURTEEN: You're too fat.

JANE: Yeah, you're right. We have to work on that. I'll work on the weight if you'll stick around and help — okay?

JANE AT FOURTEEN: Yeah . . . No ice cream, I guess?
JANE: Nope — and long walks every day.

Jane had many such conversations with her child, and soon she began to integrate into her own adult life that beautiful, imaginative young person. They also talked about doing the responsible thing, and these conversations helped Jane stop some abusive behaviors: drinking those extra glasses of wine, not getting enough sleep, eating the secretive two pints of ice cream after having had only a salad for dinner. She lost the extra weight with which she had been protecting her child. And with all of these changes came increased success as an actress.

The last time I saw Jane work, she was in a love scene. She and the man were playful with one another, but there was a clear attraction. That's not an easy kind of scene to play, but Jane was strong, funny, and interesting. She never merged with the other actor, and there was no doubt about who her character was. She clearly belonged in the scene.

Jane has been able to teach her child within that:

- It's okay to be pretty.
- Her place in the world is wherever she is, doing whatever she is doing.
- There are no hidden rules that create a pass-fail situation.
- If she is chosen, she will know exactly what is required of her.
- She has a right to respect, and others do not have the right to abuse her.

Jane continued to have the courage to ask for help — in rape counseling, from her therapist, and from her child — and her reward has been feeling that she can breathe freely for the first time in many years. Her little girl has been her guide back to who she is.

Glenn: Learning to trust

Glenn is a twenty-one-year-old drama major who lives in California. He is an only child. I first met him in an acting seminar, where he was playing a scene in which three young adults from a close-knit family were discussing their father's illness. They were supposed to be supportive of one another, and Glenn was having a lot of trouble with the scene.

He was afraid to trust people, afraid of being touched by others, and it showed in the way he played the role of one of the brothers. After the seminar Glenn asked to see me privately.

When we met I asked Glenn, "How old is the kid in you?" His response was immediate.

"Eight!"

"What was happening when you were eight?"

"We moved from the East Coast to a big midwestern city," he said. On the East Coast, everything had been wonderful. Glenn's father had traveled on business a great deal, and his mother was somewhat remote, but many of his parents' friends were like adoptive parents to him, and he was surrounded by loving, supportive people. He knew everyone, was popular at school, and felt that he belonged.

The move was a promotion for his father, a manufacturer's representative, but it meant that he would be traveling even more. When he was home he was a very demonstrative man, showering his son with presents and affection. But then he would leave. Glenn learned to equate affection with subsequent loss of affection.

From the beginning, the move was difficult for Glenn. He knew no one at the new school, and was the only new student that semester. There were several larger boys in his class who bullied and taunted him. The biggest and most frightening of these bullies was Vito.

One cold winter day, Vito and the others teased Glenn so badly that he got off the bus three stops before his house, just to get away from them. He ran through the snow, terrified that Vito might get off at the next stop and be waiting for him.

His parents had always told Glenn that if he ever needed their help, all he had to do was ask. He needed help now, and he ran as fast as he could for home.

When he arrived, he found his mother watching television. He ran to her, clung to her, and gasped, "The kids from school are after me. They hate me!"

His mother's response was, "What have you done?!"

When Glenn told me this story, his actual words were, "My mother was sitting there, watching it all, and she knew everything. But, of course, she couldn't know everything, but she . . . but she . . ." The eight-year-old Glenn believed that his mother had seen everything that had happened but chose to do nothing about it, so her betrayal was even more hurtful. Not only that, she had blamed him. By asking, "What have you done?" she had assumed that he was at fault.

The message he got was that if he did ask for help, he would not get it. He also learned that his feelings of terror would be belittled and invalidated. He already knew that feeling affection meant losing affection. He shut down many feelings that day; he would not be hurt again.

The innocent child of the first eight years grew up that winter, and from then until he was in his senior year in high school, Glenn feels that he barely survived. There are times during that period that he can't remember at all, but little things are beginning to come back. Although he is very intelligent, he just managed to scrape by in school. There were many behavior problems and lots of wild rebelliousness.

During his senior year in high school, Glenn discovered acting. He loved it, but quickly realized that it could also be quite painful. The more he went back into himself for the truth, the more it hurt. And the more experience he got, the clearer it became that his lack of trust was keeping him from being as good as he could be.

As soon as we began to work together, Glenn connected with his child and quickly bridged the gap between eight and twenty-one. The first time he worked with his eight-year-old child, he began to breathe deeply, and there was a color and warmth in his face that I'd never seen before. He began to cry for the child he had been, and for having cut himself off from his feelings.

He told his child that it was okay to trust again, and that he was going to take care of him and not let him be hurt. He let the child know that, yes, things had been very bad back then, but that it was all in the past, and now he was free to play. He told the child that it was okay to come out of his hiding place, to feel, and to do the things he'd always dreamed of doing. The child hadn't done anything wrong; it was just that Mom hadn't seen the situation clearly. He had felt abandoned by his mother, and scared of the boys, but there was nothing to be frightened of now.

Glenn's work paid off quickly. Now he gets positive reinforcement from his professors, from other actors, and in interviews and auditions arranged by his agent. He is more relaxed, and his voice has opened up. His eyes used to dart around the room as if he were searching for a way to escape; now he can hold a casting director's eyes and say that he is an actor. He is more able to enjoy both sexual and nonsexual relationships.

For Glenn, the way back involved working with a psychiatrist. He is now in the process of deciding whether he really wants to act professionally, or whether he would rather become an agent or perhaps a casting director. In both of these professions he would be working with actors but would be a step removed from the responsibility of being "the creative one." Every creative arena has people who don't really want this kind of responsibility but who turn out to be great agents or teachers because they have such an intimate understanding of the process.

Regardless of what Glenn chooses, he has recovered the truest part of himself.

Fulfilling the Needs of the Child Within

Finding the child within requires patience and imagination. Some of these children are eager to be found; others, shy and frightened, need to be coaxed out.

Each child needs to be parented differently; only we can know what the missing ingredients are and how to give them to our child.

The case studies in this chapter present a variety of approaches to finding and parenting the child within, but there are common elements, certain things that each child needs. These are the things that were denied us when we were young and that help the child lead us back to ourselves and our creative center.

The child within us needs:

- An apology for having abandoned him or her and a promise to try not to do it again.
- The chance to describe how the child felt back then.
- Unconditional acceptance — permission from ourselves to ourselves to be exactly as we are and to express that essence in the world.
- Unconditional love, no matter what we say or do.
- Encouragement to trust ourselves and other people, to feel safe because our adult selves are now there to protect the child.
- Permission to play and to relax.
- Reminders that what happened back then is in the past, and that we can create our own present and future.
- A promise that we will never let the child be hurt again.

Most of us have been waiting all our lives for someone to give us these things, and nobody ever will. No one can do these things for us; we have to do them for ourselves. All the child within us wants is for us to put our arms around him or her and say, "I love you, and I'll take care of you."

Trusting the Wisdom of the Child Within

How do we know that the child-voice to which we learn to listen is wise and can be trusted? It feels right, but how do we know that it *is* right?

David, the client whose letter to his father appears in Chapter Four, is a thoughtful and religious man. He asked me where I thought the voice of the child, who had become so important to him, would fit into his religious beliefs. His question was, "Whose voice is this?"

At first, the voice of the child within him was something he used only in his acting — to solve problems; to enable him to have more fun, laughter, and play; and to keep him focused on a scene.

But gradually this "internal child" had become more and more powerful, active in other areas of his life as well.

David spent a great deal of time and energy bringing his child into the present, and he said, "It really works for me. It has solved problems, gives me comfort and answers. It has brought fun and laughter back into my life and work, but the closer I get to the kid, the essence of who I am, the more I wonder where all this fits into my belief in God and my religion."

Our search for answers to his question led us through conversations ranging over vast areas of both our lives. We agreed that church dogma or belief—the "laws" of a religion—indicates the way that we are to live in the world. This seems to apply no matter what the religion or how general or specific, formal or informal a belief system one might have.

Finally we came to believe that the child-voice is, in a sense, our personal god-voice or guide, our Buddha nature, our messenger from the greater consciousness or universe. This child-voice is our connection to a source of *internal* wisdom, as contrasted to the *external* belief system of a church.

Living a creative life is rather like traveling on an express train facing backwards. We can see where we have been, but we cannot see into the future. Everyone's life is like this, but people in the creative professions have even fewer clear directions than most others. If we cannot know everything that is to happen, the progress of our work must be shaped by faith. When we feel that each piece of our work is part of a larger whole and that our life in turn has its place in the continuum of human experience, then we have a sense of coming home, of being alive, vibrant, and at peace. We have the feeling that everything we're doing is working in harmony and that we are doing what we were placed here to do. Whatever our religious belief or lack of it, this sense of harmony lets us know that we are part of the infinite, which curiously is part of ourselves. When we listen to the child-voice, we find our place in this world. We belong. We have come home to ourselves.

chapter 4
The Power of Writing

Memory changes with time. Events are colored by feelings, enhanced by imagined promises or hopes, obscured by the passing years. When time and emotions are involved, it is often difficult to recall events as they actually happened.

Remembering how we felt during an interview, a class, or a rehearsal seems fairly simple. But if we are asked to recall a whole history of interviews, classes, or rehearsals over a period of three to six months, for instance, in order to gain perspective on how our career has evolved — or failed to evolve — that is more difficult.

Writing things down can help us see what actually happened and understand how we traveled from point A to point B. It can also be a powerful tool in locating and working through our blocks.

We learn most about ourselves when we write what we *feel*, rather than what we *think*.

My clients have found three kinds of writing exercises to be particularly helpful:

1. Class, audition, and agent journals
2. Lists
3. Letters to the past that release stuck emotions

We all have different relationships with writing. For some, it is as natural as breathing; for others, it is extremely difficult. Some people find it the most helpful tool they have ever encountered; others find that other forms of expression bring them closer to their true feelings. By experimenting, we learn which tools work best for us.

How Journals Help

A journal that includes feelings as well as thoughts can be a valuable record that allows us to look back over weeks, months, or even years to discover patterns of feelings and behaviors. This helps us not only to identify blocks but also to understand them and see what we need to do about them. Journals show us precisely the path we have walked, and whether or not we are heading in the direction we want to go.

From the journal, we learn to see what works and what doesn't work. We may have been doing something particularly destructive, or particularly brilliant, all along—but without the journal we might never know it. Without an exact record of what happened, it is much more difficult to perceive patterns in our behavior; it may seem as though a certain experience "just keeps happening" to us.

By reading over these journals, noticing the words we have chosen, and recreating what we felt at certain points in the class, audition, or interview, we can gain new insight into what triggers us and how we are apt to react in certain situations.

For instance, journals have helped many of my clients pinpoint where their fear of performing comes from and have shown them how to deal with it. Roger said to me, "In this class I'm taking, everything is fine until it gets close to my turn. Then I start to panic and, by the time it's my turn, I'm hardly even conscious of what I'm doing. It happens every time. I'm thinking that maybe I should drop the class."

I asked Roger to keep a journal of the class, using the techniques described in this chapter. Within three weeks, he was able to look back and see what had happened in each small slice of time as the class progressed; this showed him the components of the panic attacks and exactly what they felt like.

Roger's panic centered around the issue of being judged—a part of his life as an actor that had always bothered him. Our discussions about the journal he had written revealed that he felt the same panic with casting directors; he feared that they were judging him and that he would be found wanting. Roger's mother had been loving and gentle, his father and grandfather remote and judgmental. He felt that the standards had always been moved further away from his achievements, so that no matter what he did or how hard he tried, he could never attain what his father and grandfather wanted of him. He was now allowing the teacher of his acting class to assume their role. He even jokingly said that he had taken this particular class because the teacher was a woman and maybe she would be easier to work with, but it hadn't worked out that way. The class standards were high, and Roger's old feelings had returned. Even when he knew that he had prepared correctly for class, he felt that it would somehow turn out to be wrong.

Part of Roger's work involved the inner child, and part simply had to do with recognizing where this feeling that he could never do well came from. Now, as it gets near his turn in class, he reminds himself that this is a place for discovering things, for taking risks and finding out how things work, and that some judging is necessary so that his work can grow. He uses various relaxing techniques, including deep breathing and staying centered in his body as he breathes, rubbing his hands gently over his legs and being aware of the sensations—all aimed at staying present in the moment with himself. If panic starts to creep in, he writes in his notebook, "Hello, panic, I don't need you right now—I've got more important things to attend to." And he reassures the child within that it's okay, that nothing bad is going to happen.

Every actor has these feelings of panic at some point. Part of the problem lies in believing that fear is something that happens *to* us. In fact, we play an active part in the situations where we feel fear, and the past is usually involved in determining how fearful we are. Even though these panic attacks seem to be caused by circumstances over which we have no control, we do have power over at least one element in the drama: our own reactions. But we have to recognize these reactions before we can do anything to change them — and that's where the journal comes in.

The Class Journal

The class journal is different from the notes we take in class on what the instructor says. This journal is a notebook in which we jot down feelings, upsets, high moments, or any other important emotions that occur during class. If something another person says or does triggers fear, anger, or some other strong emotion, we write it down in the class journal. We don't have to stop and unravel the whole tangle of emotional history behind this reaction right there in the middle of class; we just scribble down the essence of the feeling in a word or two. It's important for the entries to begin "I felt," not "I thought."

When class is over, we can take another few minutes to write down how we felt in general during the class and how we feel about it now that it's over. It doesn't matter how the journal looks, how illogical it may seem, or how embarrassing it is. These notes are for our eyes only.

Obviously, in the journal, we want to be as honest as we can about our feelings. Here's an example from the notes my client Marie wrote after one of her classes: "When HE [the instructor] let that other actor really have it because he hadn't learned his lines, I felt like I used to feel in Mrs. MacPherson's English class. She hated me and I hated her. I began to feel that the instructor hated me, and even though I knew I had prepared well for the class, somehow I would not know my lines either, and then the instructor would really hate me. This in spite of the fact that I like him, and he has said some good things about my work."

These feelings may be very important to Marie's acting — or completely unimportant. All we know from this one class is that the feelings came up. If the associations with Mrs. MacPherson and the fear of being hated come up several times, then Marie may need to look at what role Mrs. MacPherson played in her early years and determine how the feeling that this teacher hated her is affecting her present life and work. Once the problem is identified, she can start to work on it.

After we have written our postclass notes, we should go back to the few words we scribbled in class and make sure that those moments have been included. They are frequently danger flags, so if they have not been included, it is important to examine them in more detail and write about them fully. Take a few moments to allow them to float around inside you in an aimless sort of way. Where do they end up? Maybe nowhere important, or maybe they trigger an "ah-ha" moment that bears further examination. Marie, for example, might remember something specific about Mrs. MacPherson that will be useful to her.

Next we should take a moment to evaluate the work we did in class. My client Andrew in New York wrote, "I knew what I was going to do and I did it. I felt more comfortable, and mostly what I wanted was what I did. I felt better than last week, but I still felt that Jerry was better. I think the instructor thought Jerry was better than I was."

Andrew fell into the trap of comparing himself to another actor. Even though a part of him was satisfied with the work he'd done, he let the comparison color his evaluation of his own work and distract him from his own progress and achievement. It's important to validate each step we take, no matter how small or unimportant it may seem.

When Andrew read over his notes, he recognized his tendency to compare himself with others. This recognition gave him an edge; now he could put some effort into understanding where the habit came from so that he could break it. Armed with the information that he compares himself unfavorably to others, Andrew remembered that in his family his achievements were always compared with those of his cousin, who was two years older. Andrew needed to remind himself that no one in his family had ever been an actor before, that there was no family standard to measure up to, and that he was as different from Jerry as he was from his cousin. Without the journal, Andrew might never have noticed his habit of making negative comparisons.

Jody, a Denver actress, discovered from reading over her class journal why she never did her best work in class. She found several journal entries along the lines of "I felt uncentered and distracted before I started. I was still thinking about the scene Cheryl had done. It was moving, but I would have done it a little differently." In other words, she would get so absorbed in watching other people work that she was still involved in their performances when it was her turn to do her scene.

It takes time to gather our concentration and center ourselves. We need to take that time *before* we go onstage or in front of the camera. We learn from watching other people, but there are times when we have to concentrate solely on our own work. Maybe we need time to talk with our child, to remind him or her that the instructor is not our parent or football coach or dance teacher. We should take whatever time we need in order to do our best work.

Looking over journal entries from five or six classes will reveal immediately what our patterns are and what is working or not working about our approach to the class. Then what?

There are several steps we can take.

1. Write further about these patterns, concentrating on what we feel about them, how we believe they evolved, and what we want to do about them.
2. Work like a detective on our own behalf, watching out for the patterns, stopping ourselves if we start to tumble into them again, and constantly reassuring the child within.
3. See a therapist, perhaps bringing our discoveries to each session and working on these issues.
4. Confide in another student or another actor with whom we feel comfortable, inviting that person to share his or her fears and stumbling blocks with us as well. Simply talking about such fears often makes them less powerful. If this person is someone in the same class, we can ask him or her to watch for certain things in our work and discuss them after class. The instructor may also be willing to help in this way. We might say, for instance, "I'm going through some real

changes. I know that I put a mask on when I'm uncertain. Would you please tell me whenever you see that mask being put in place?" Now we have opened the door to talking with an ally about what is getting in the way of our work.

It's hard to evaluate our own work. If comments from other students and the instructor agree, but are different from our own perceptions, perhaps we are not being entirely objective. We need to consider whether others are on to something that we can't see. Perhaps we might start making journal notes about this issue.

The most important step in keeping a class journal involves putting these discoveries to work for us. We may feel uncomfortable at first as we try to change old patterns and habits. If we have been fighting against allowing our vulnerability to show, for instance, it may feel quite strange the first few times we succeed in doing so. To those watching, it will probably be magical. To us, it may feel unlike anything we have experienced before.

The Danger of Taking Too Many Notes in Class

It's possible to take so many class notes that we become more involved with the process of writing than we are with our own reactions and what is actually going on in the room. Jean took one of my workshops, and she looked up from her notes so seldom that I wondered if she was really getting what I was saying.

Jean was very intelligent and thorough, but she came from a background in which one did not show emotions. Her acting could be wonderful, but the rehearsal process was difficult for her. She felt she had to get everything exactly right before she showed it in public, even if it was just a scene for class or rehearsal. It was difficult for her to open up and let people see the "work in progress."

In this particular workshop she wrote down every comment I made on her work, but there would be very little difference the next time she did the scene. It was as if my comments had become lodged in her left brain and were not available to her in emotional form when she needed them.

When I asked Jean what she did with all her notes, she said she almost never read them over. She agreed that for the rest of the workshop, she would try to experience what I was saying, rather than writing it all down. Not being able to hide behind her pencil and paper made her feel so vulnerable that she could hardly even hear what I was saying. She felt completely exposed. It was uncomfortable at the time, but even that brief exercise opened up something special in her acting.

In a letter she wrote to me after the class was over, Jean said, "I realized, after the workshop, that I used note taking sometimes as an excuse to avoid interaction with people, and I'm working on it. I have a lot of head knowledge about acting. Now it is transferring it to the gut that I need to work on."

In addition to the brief notes jotted down in a class journal, there are, of course, other things that need to be written down — things that are so important that they belong in large letters on walls or mirrors. Sometimes a director or teacher says something that makes light bulbs light up, or he or she offers a simple explanation that clears up years of confusion. We need to extract such notes from our journals and pin them above our desk or on the refrigerator so that they become part of our thinking. Michel St. Denis's "What is the truth, dear chap, the truth?" was such a note for me. "Acting is the sharing of secrets" and "Reality does not discuss, it simply is" are others that have spent time on the wall above my desk.

The Audition and Interview Journals

Many of the same principles and steps described for class journals also apply to keeping audition and interview journals, but obviously the stakes are higher and some of the gremlins that appear in class journals may loom even larger here. This fact makes audition and interview journals even more valuable for identifying blocks and for working on getting rid of them.

After each audition or interview, we need to take some time alone to write down how we felt about it, including anything stressful that happened just before the event: getting caught in a traffic jam, being late and having to rush, having trouble parking, experiencing horrors on the subway, how we felt walking in the door, what happened in the reception area, and anything else that might have caused tension.

If we have patterns that make the arrival part of the interview or audition more difficult than it needs to be, they are actually quite simple to change. If we are often late, for instance, we can plan to be half an hour early and take a book to enjoy during the wait. If the journal reflects that we feel great when we leave home but then get involved in competitive chatter with other actors in the reception area and lose our confidence, we can find ways of avoiding that pattern: reading a book or magazine, writing in the journal, anything that keeps us centered and out of those conversations. Or our child may get agitated in stressful or competitive situations, and we may need to give him or her some special care and attention.

After writing down how we felt during the audition or interview, it's interesting to note whether or not we felt that we would get the role, and whether we felt it was right for us. From how the character was described (age, demeanor, station in life, and so on), would the role have been a real stretch, or did it feel easy?

If we find out who actually did get the role, we can make a note of that as well. It's also good to note whether or not we were called back, along with any information from our agent about what the casting director thought. This gives us information about what kinds of roles we actually get, what kinds of roles the agent thinks of us for, and, to some extent, what casting directors think of our work.

If we have a pattern of thinking that we did badly, but then are called back or get the part, perhaps we should stop worrying so much when we feel dissatisfied with an audition. It might also be worthwhile to explore why we feel that we don't do good work when others think we do. We may be programmed to feel that we have to be "perfect," an issue that we will examine in the Epilogue.

Finally, if we feel that we did a good job in the audition, yet we still were not cast, we must honor our own assessment of our work. We can never hear it too often: There are other considerations besides the quality of our work that go into casting decisions, and even our best work cannot guarantee that we will be cast. It helps to think of auditions and interviews as opportunities in themselves for practicing our craft; they *are* "our work."

The Agent Journal

Another type of journal, slightly different from the others, is the one we keep on meetings with our agent. The actor-agent relationship can be a challenging one, and it involves a tremendous amount of trust on both sides.

Technically, the actor is the one hiring and paying the agent, but in many ways the agent has all the power because he or she controls the actor's access to work. Actors feel that they need to stay in their agents' good graces, and they have a tendency to do whatever their agents say without question.

We should meet with our agent periodically to discuss where our career is going. Audition and interview journals can be an enormous help in these discussions because they provide a record of the number of auditions we've had and the roles for which we've auditioned, been called back, and been hired. These journals tell us if we have read ten times for the role of a cop and have not been cast once, even though we felt the readings were good. They tell us whether we got cast every time we read for a teacher, the vice-president of a company, or an administrative assistant. They tell us if we have read twenty times for the same casting director and have been turned down every time.

This is valuable information; sharing it with the agent can help him or her do a better job. It opens up a discussion about the next steps in our career, where we are most likely to be cast, and why. If we are well informed, we can also be more assertive, and these meetings with the agent will be more productive.

After each meeting, we should write down what was said and what decisions were made, especially noting issues on which we're not yet clear. We shouldn't hesitate to call the agent to clarify anything that's still fuzzy. Referring to these notes before the next meeting will help us to identify what we want and to hear clearly what the agent says.

If our relationship with the agent isn't what we want it to be, we should note all our interactions with him or her in the journal: phone calls, personal meetings, and letters. As with the other kinds of journals, the entries should start with "I felt," not with "I thought." Soon a pattern will emerge in the journal.

Sometimes there isn't much to say to an agent except "Thank you, I'll be there" or "Thank you, I'll pick up the script." It's not necessary to trade witticisms each time we speak with him or her. People who are on the phone all day, as agents are, appreciate working with clients who listen, get the information right, and sound as if they appreciate what is being done in their behalf.

An agent is not a therapist or a parent. It is not his or her job to take care of our psychological needs. Clients who need a great deal of emotional support from their agents put them in an awkward position. The agent doesn't have the time or the training to handle these needs. Every minute spent holding an actor's hand is a minute taken away from trying to get that actor work. Emotional support has to come from sources other than the agent: therapists, groups, friends, ourselves, this book — whatever works for us.

Lists

Many actors get so overwhelmed by the enormity of what is before them — "becoming a success," "moving my career forward," "making it" — that they become paralyzed. One way to free ourselves from this tension is to make a list of "to do's" that is finite and manageable, not an endless stream of tasks without boundaries or end points.

Each "to do" should be specific. For instance, we wouldn't put on the list "Become a wonderful actress," but we might include "Learn the new monologue," "Spend an hour working with the camera," "Make a date with Judy to rehearse two hours next week," or "Learn the new dance routine."

Whether we are plotting a career, organizing the next month, or figuring out what has to get done today, making a list can be an enormous help for three reasons:

1. Writing down what we need to do for our work dignifies that work and elevates it to the stature it must have in order to flourish.
2. Lists keep us organized and focused, headed in the direction we have chosen.
3. Writing things down frees the brain for more important work. It's hard to be creative when we're trying to remember everything we have to do in the next week, or that we have to pick up coffee, onions, and paper towels on the way home. Writing these things down lets us stop thinking about them. We can let the piece of paper hold them; our minds were made for better things.

Sally: Ruling her lists or being ruled by them

Lists only help if we don't become slaves to them. If my client Sally had on her list "Work on the new scene," she would do it because her life was completely organized around her lists. But she gave creative work a lower priority than other items, so she often wound up rehearsing between eleven at night and two in the morning, when her energy and enthusiasm were waning and concentration was difficult. She didn't get much joy or satisfaction from her work under those circumstances, even though she could cross that item off her list.

We had to look to the past to discover why Sally used her lists to control her life. She had known in her teens that she wanted to be a professional pianist. Her art had required a great deal of discipline and concentration, and so much of her time was taken up with lessons and practice that she didn't have much contact with friends her own age. Sally's father, who disapproved of her choice, told her that she'd be playing in piano bars within five years. He was a strict disciplinarian and had been physically violent with her when she was younger.

Sally's mother, on the other hand, had done everything for her. Until she left home for college, Sally didn't even know how to do laundry. All she had ever done was go to school, take piano lessons, practice many hours a day, perform in concerts, and compete in contests.

As a result, Sally had become totally dependent on one parent and totally alienated from the other. As an adult, she used her lists to recreate both her mother's and her father's roles. The lists helped her do the caretaking things her mother had always done for her, such as laundry, grocery shopping, and housekeeping. But if she failed to complete every task on her list, she berated herself as her father would have done.

Sally's list making also gave her life the rigid control she felt she needed to keep it from falling apart. As a teenager and at the beginning of her professional career, she had had a piano teacher who had taught her the joy and freedom of doing what she was meant to do. There was no sexual involvement, but Sally had cared more for this loving teacher than for her own parents, and this had made her feel guilty.

By the time Sally graduated from high school, she was already having a great deal of success — she had won several awards and competitions — but her father became so jealous of her teacher that eventually the lessons and performances were discontinued, and Sally gave up the piano. At that point the equation of love, freedom, and relaxation with disaster was complete. In college Sally changed her focus to acting, but the same blocks cropped up in her second career as well.

Sally's feelings were very confused. Approval and disapproval were inextricably linked in her mind. The same commitment to her piano that had gained her teacher's approval had prompted her father's disapproval. Her list making became a way to win both approval (for what she managed to get done) and disapproval (for what she did not).

After graduation from college, she married a rich, protective, and understanding man. Her grasp of the "real" world was tenuous at this point — she was, after all, just learning to do laundry — and in an attempt to keep some kind of balance between the household and acting, she began to make even more exhaustive and demanding lists and to follow them even more compulsively. For a while this worked, but ultimately it produced the rigidity that brought her to me.

When I first started working with Sally, her hair, makeup, and clothes were incredibly neat and meticulous. Her acting was the same way. Everything in her life was "listed." She felt that if she could just do everything on her list, then she would be a successful actress.

In reality, the items that concerned acting were seldom even started, let alone completed. Anything to do with acting was relegated to a lower position than household duties, below picking up the cleaning, buying dog food, and getting the car washed.

"I drive myself nuts trying to do everything. Everything is important, and I have to do everything," she said with determination.

She scarcely heard me when I said, "Wrong . . . wrong . . ."

"I try to make everybody happy and I can't. It's hard to decide how to balance everything out because I want to do everything. My career is the most important thing now, it seems like, but thank goodness my husband is gone a lot because I get more work done when he's gone . . . but, you know, life is just tough, I guess. I don't know . . . there are just so many things to do. You never run out of things . . . I have to learn how to make better lists, or maybe more lists. I only have five."

"You have five lists?"

"Yes, of course. I have to keep organized and find my priorities."

"What do you do when you don't get through the lists?"

"Oh, I get frustrated, and I keep them for another day."

"Do you ever throw a list away?"

"Throw it away?"

"Yes, throw it away."

She was baffled. "No! Then I wouldn't remember what it was I had to do later."

I asked Sally if she felt that all the uncompleted lists gave her a way to judge herself.

"Well, yes." She shook her finger: "'You didn't do everything you were supposed to.'"

I suggested that she try making two different, shorter lists — one of things she really wanted to do and the other of things she really had to do. If she did one thing from the second list, then she also had to do one thing from the first list.

"That's a great idea," she said. "Why didn't I think of that? I feel freer just thinking about it! Maybe I wouldn't feel so rigid. I've been having problems with stress, stomach problems, lots of tense muscles. I guess it comes from me and my lists, trying to be perfect for everyone."

Sally was silent for a few minutes, and then she placed her hands gently on her stomach. "You know, I feel things loosening up inside already. Maybe I *can* change things. I need to talk to other people, to get them to feel that my work, my being an actress, is important."

Sally always comes to our sessions with a list of what she wants to talk about, which is a productive use of list making. She used to get very frustrated if we didn't get to everything in order, but now she can relax and trust that we will cover what we need to cover.

She has taken giant strides as an actress, largely because she has given herself permission to spend time with some acting coaches to whom she relates as she did to her old piano teacher. They have helped her to gain the freedom and joy that had been lacking in her work.

Sally realized that she had been using her lists to distance herself from what she really wanted to do. The last time she had done what she really wanted — excelled as a pianist — it had ended in disaster, and she was afraid that her acting would end the same way. When she became aware of this subconscious association, she was able to do something about it so that she could move forward.

Letters to the Past

Writing letters to the past can be a tremendous release. Sometimes it's just too painful to talk about our feelings, and the best way to get them unstuck and flowing out of us is to put them down on paper. Often we can write about things that we can't yet say out loud. Even when verbal interaction is out of the question — either because the people involved are no longer living or because a face-to-face encounter would be too painful or even dangerous — we can write letters to the people with whom we need to communicate.

In these letters, we tell people the things we've always been too afraid, angry, or confused to tell them. The people might be our parents, our relatives, or a coach or teacher — anyone with whom we associate those early hurts and fears.

We don't send the letters, because we need to be able to say *anything*, no matter how terrible or inappropriate, in order to get to the truth. We need to be able to write in an uncensored way, without concern for other people's feelings or for the consequences. It often takes several of these "dumping" letters before what we really want to say begins to emerge.

The important thing is to start releasing the emotions attached to the past, getting them out so that we don't have to carry them around inside us for the rest of our lives.

These letters are about feelings and emotions, not thoughts or opinions. The key, as in the journals, is to begin sentences with "I feel," not "I think."

Leslie: Working through trauma

Leslie is twenty-four years old and lives in New York, but she was brought up in a wealthy family in the Southeast. When she made her first appointment to see me, she said that she was confused about what roles she should play and what she should audition for. I asked her what kind of roles felt right to her.

"At one point I thought I knew that," she replied, "but somehow I seem to have lost track of it."

When I asked her if she knew when the confusion had started, she said that she didn't remember, and anyway, she couldn't talk about "all that."

"All that" turned out to be the previous six years of her life, which had been filled with tragedy and trauma.

As Leslie was growing up, she had received from her mother a clearly defined picture of what her life should look like: Leslie would marry a professional man, preferably a doctor, and live a comfortable, respectable life.

Doing what pleased her mother had always meant a great deal to Leslie, and at eighteen she moved in with a doctor, Carlton, who was twenty-five years her senior. Her mother was thrilled, although she would have been more thrilled if they'd been married. Carlton was successful socially and professionally, but he was also addicted to drugs and alcohol. He would vanish for days at a time, and he abused Leslie both physically and mentally.

While Leslie was living with Carlton, he tried twice to commit suicide. Each attempt left Leslie feeling that it was her fault. She didn't know what she was supposed to be to him, or what she was supposed to do to make him want to live, but obviously she was failing. She tried everything she knew to make him happy and to keep him from killing himself. It never occurred to her that this gave him tremendous power over her. Nor did it occur to her that his suicide attempts were not her fault. She didn't feel that she could talk to anyone about the problem.

When I asked Leslie how old her child was, she replied, "Fourteen." Up until that point in our conversation, her face had been very set and determined. Suddenly, the most delightful smile crinkled around her mouth and eyes, and she laughed. "I guess I had more fun then than I've ever had." She talked about her friends, about her school, and also about the fact that around that time she had discovered that she was a lesbian. She had not shared this discovery with her family; she hadn't even thought much about what it implied in terms of her mother's plans for her.

After living with Carlton for about eighteen months, Leslie became interested in a woman named Natalie, who lived over a thousand miles away. Even though she saw Natalie only occasionally, their friendship precipitated many fights between Leslie and Carlton, and some ugly teasing on his part about "Who do you like best?"

Finally, Leslie couldn't take it anymore. She and Carlton separated, although they remained friends, running together twice a week. Within three months, Carlton was living with an eighteen-year-old woman.

One night he and Leslie were talking on the phone, and he pressed her again on the question of whether she liked him or Natalie best. Reluctantly, Leslie answered that she preferred Natalie. The next morning they were to run together, but Leslie's car battery was dead, and she was late to meet him. Carlton arrived at the track on time, and there he shot himself. Leslie believes that he intended to kill her and then himself.

Leslie decided never to talk about Carlton's death, and had kept all the anger and grief bottled up for three years. During that time she had received no counseling or professional support; instead, she had thrown herself into acting as a release. But as time passed, she found that there were certain scenes she couldn't do, certain scenes she felt were actually dangerous to her. Being asked to recreate some emotions was so painful that she finally realized she needed help.

Holding on that tightly, keeping herself on such a short rein, had resulted in the feeling that she would never be free again, that she could never relax, that her options in life were extremely limited, and that her horizons were shrinking rather than expanding. In real life, she had played the role she had thought she was meant to play, and it had ended horribly. No wonder she was confused about which roles to play as an actress.

All the things she had felt at fourteen — the freedom, the laughter, the confidence, the sense that she could do or be anything she wanted — had been shut down. That free spirit had disappeared and been replaced by a grim young woman with little self-esteem, a woman who seemed closer to age fifty than to twenty-four. This was the woman who had denied her own needs and instincts and had knuckled under to her mother's plans for her. Her acting teachers often commented on her remoteness, on her lack of spontaneity and involvement, and on how much older than her actual age she appeared in her work.

Leslie got involved in grief counseling and therapy and also began writing letters to the past: to her mother and the other people who had designed her life for her, to her teachers, to friends whom she felt had never understood her, and finally to Carlton.

The letter to Carlton was written several years ago, when Leslie's feelings were still quite raw. At that point, it was a tremendous relief for her. She has kept the letter and reads it over occasionally to gauge her progress. She now sees not only how self-destructive her behavior was when she was with him, but how angry she was years later when she wrote the letter. She also sees how much higher her self-esteem is today, and knows that she will never put herself in a similar position again.

This is what she wrote to Carlton, three years after his death:

Dear Carlton,

It's taken me a long time to write this letter. My mother suggested it to me after she saw a special on television where Katharine Hepburn read a letter she had written to Spencer Tracy, eighteen years after he died. I kept thinking that I would write to you. Tonight I caught the end of that same tribute to Spence when Katharine read the letter. I just finished *A Remarkable Woman,* too. It's a biography about Katharine, so I learned a lot about Katharine's and Spence's relationship. He was an alcoholic, too, and would disappear for days on end like you did, and Kate could track him down like I could track you.

Remember when we took our first trip away together? I was getting out of the shower and you yelled to me that there was a Katharine Hepburn movie on and there was one woman that you would love to go to bed with. I remarked quite seriously, "So would I." You laughed and laughed.

There is not a day that I don't think about you and cry about you. It usually happens when I'm doing something that we liked to do together. Oh, it could be almost any-thing. I'm just floating through life, waiting. It feels like when I would wait for you to come home from the office, or wait for you to come back after disappearing for a few days. I was always afraid you were dead. Now you are. And

I am still waiting. You still make me cry every day. I can't
look around my home without seeing or touching something we bought or you gave me. I was just telling a friend
about the piece we found and bought. I never know what
to call it; I guess I will call it a cloth relief. Anyway, I was
saying that the lion was you, and that the unicorn represented women, and my friend said that I was the human
woman [in the middle] balancing the energies by resting
my hands on their heads. The lion really looks like you—
long, flowing mane. Even your profiles are the same.

The lion is a symbol of courage, though. I told you
both times you tried to commit suicide that it was cowar-
dice. Why was living so hard for you? I'm glad I told you I
loved you before you tried it this last time. You wouldn't
do anything for yourself. People don't care that you were a
doctor who lost interest in his practice, then lost his practice and everything material that came with it. You could
have started over, just changed your life. Change is what
life is about.

But you wouldn't know about that now. I am trying to
change, be something more, be ambitious, be focused, be
happy, etc. It's been hard, because I thought I was worth
nothing. I am working on that now with my analyst. Yes,
Carlton, she is an M.D.

Leslie

When Leslie first wrote this letter, she felt a tremendous sense
of release. The pressure that had been building up inside her
started to dissipate. A year later, I asked her to reread it. She
stopped when she got to the part about feeling worthless. "I
wrote that?" she asked. "I don't feel worthless anymore." She saw
that that period in her life was receding into the past.

Leslie had always been afraid that if she ever let herself feel
again, the emotions would be overpowering. She thought she
might have a breakdown if they raged out of control. Writing
these letters and working with a therapist gave Leslie access to
her emotions again. She began to realize that she could safely

experience, both in her life and in her work as an actress, some of the feelings that she had put on hold.

Leslie keeps all her old letters in a file, to which she refers whenever she needs access to those feelings for a character. She can go to those files without being swallowed up by emotion. She can take away with her just enough anger, just enough tears, just enough sense of loss to create the moments she needs. She is back in charge. She has become more vulnerable, and she no longer feels that she can play only certain kinds of scenes.

I often urge my clients to do what Leslie did and file their letters away in a place that is difficult to reach — behind something, on top of something, under something that has to be moved. Putting these sheets of paper away is a physical acting out of the idea of putting the old hurts away. It also reinforces the image of creating an emotional savings account. A wide range of emotions can be filed away, and we can later make "withdrawals" in any amount we choose. The feelings are available to us at any time, but we no longer have to carry them around inside us.

Leslie found that working through these feelings also solved another, less important problem. Whenever a teacher, director, or casting director asked Leslie a question, she used to blush uncontrollably. She always felt that she was hiding something, and that the other person was about to find out what it was. As she got some of her "hidden" feelings about the past out on paper, the blushing became more manageable.

Leslie's letters to the past didn't solve all her problems, and they were not the sole component in her healing, but they did start the process and let her see that she didn't have to feel so inadequate and confused. They opened a door for her, and she had the courage to walk through it.

Lizzie: Starting the process

In the first few letters we write, we want the emotions to come spilling out without our editing them, without our having to be responsible or reasoned. These letters usually contain a great deal of blame mixed with a lot of venom, tears, anger, and love. This is as it should be; the important thing is to let the emotions out in a kind of explosion, to release them so that they can be worked through. These letters get the process started; there is plenty of time later to be responsible and to look closely at our patterns.

Sometimes these first letters don't make much sense; they may even contradict themselves. But they contain our own unique perceptions of events, and those are the perceptions on which our feelings are based. We need to give these feelings credence and respect.

Lizzie is an actress in the Midwest with an exceptional breadth of color in her work. She is enchanting to watch, but her career has been spasmodic. She gets a lot of work and is on the way to becoming well known and then stops acting for other pursuits, some of them family oriented and some that are harder to understand. She told me that whenever she began to feel she really belonged as an actress she became uncomfortable and ill at ease on a level that was scarcely tolerable. To make herself feel better she stopped acting, but then she always got ill and depressed. It would take months before she found the courage to seek work again. She said, "It is almost impossible for me to believe with any consistency that I am the actress people want. Maybe once in a while, but not all the time. I just can't believe it. I know it will come to an end, so I end it before something else does."

We started to examine why success in her work made her behave as it did, and the following is her first letter to her parents.

Dear Mom and Dad,
    Here I sit at eleven at night wondering why you never loved me. What did I do that was so bad?
    I was a girl and you wanted a boy.
    I was fat and you wanted thin.
    I was thin and you wanted heavier.
    I could never live up to your expectations.
    Now I am thirty years old and I want to be a little girl and be held and loved and kissed and told I'm all right.

Why did you have to beat me, Dad, and why couldn't you bring yourself to save me, Mom? I hate you both, and now you're both dead and I can't resolve this with *you*.

Mom, you hated me in the womb. And then I was born a girl instead of a boy. That was just the beginning of never measuring up. I could never meet your expectations.

I have to learn to hold myself and take care of the little girl who just wanted to fit in, who just wanted to be loved. I have a family now, and I need to learn to hold little Lizzie so that I can love them.

Lizzie, come out and let me hold you, because I love you.

All I have is myself and my Lord. He knows me and He loves me. With His help, I can learn to love and hold myself.

Lizzie

After writing this letter, and others like it, Lizzie began working with a therapist. Soon she started to understand that never measuring up was a part of her past, not her present. This theme, of not being good enough, had been a major issue in her acting. She is one of the most interesting actresses I have ever seen, but she never felt that there were any roles for her. As she said in the letter, she never felt that she could meet expectations. She still feels occasionally that she is wrong or unsuitable in some way, but now she knows where that feeling comes from and what to do about it. She can talk to her child and reassure her.

Lizzie often uses her letters to the past to prepare for roles. She has faced, understood, and worked through these emotions, so she isn't afraid to let the camera or the audience see her vulnerability and suffering. Her work always had a certain power, but it was erratic, and Lizzie never knew when inspiration would hit. Now she knows how to find that power and use it at will.

David: Unlocking feelings

David is an engineering consultant in southern California who has developed a very successful second career as an actor. The second of three children, he grew up in a small town in Oregon, where his family still lives. His parents are divorced, and his father has remarried. He is in his midthirties, and has never married.

David was constantly beaten and abused by his mother until he started high school. Because she didn't abuse her other children, David felt that he must have done something to deserve her wrath. The physical abuse stopped when he began high school, partly because of his size and maturity and partly because his mother resumed her career as a teacher and became much less frustrated and unhappy.

David came to see me because he felt "locked up." It was a mystery to him how others were able to let go and enjoy acting, and how anyone could have enjoyable relationships. On videotape, his face betrayed no emotion at all; it was simply a rigid mask.

As part of our work together, David began to write letters to the past, and he now has fat files of these letters — a well-stocked savings account of material from which to make withdrawals. Recently he has started writing — and sending — letters to his mother based on material from those files. As a result, they have begun to weave a new relationship.

He is now doing the same thing with his father. The following is a recent letter to his father, drawn from the material in his files. It took several drafts before David arrived at the letter that he actually sent, and since that time his feelings have evolved even further. He has come to deeper levels of understanding and forgiveness; but before he could get there, he had to tell the truth about where he was at the time he wrote the letter. Courageously, he mailed the letter before a visit home; the result was a series of long discussions and the beginning of a new honesty with his father.

Dad,

Wanted to wish you a special Father's Day. Seems unbelievable that you are retiring this year.

Sometimes looking back on my time at home is strange. I guess that's normal considering how I grew up. My childhood and college days were not so happy, but high school was great. College was the appearance of happiness but I didn't enjoy it, living in my own hometown while going through later adolescence. I guess I was a model kid in junior and senior high school, but I was not happy before junior high. Mom was an ogre, but finally got her act together when she started teaching. I still carry some of the scars from the way she treated me, and I have blamed her all my life for some of my problems, including my seeming inability to allow a woman to love me without a fight, even when I love her. I think I am getting over that and I am also getting over blaming Mom for my problems.

She didn't have it easy raising three kids, two boys a year apart with no parents to help, and you have to admit that you didn't help her much. You were out drinking, and also out with other women frequently. Mom didn't get much of a break away from us "ornery kids." When you'd come home, we were sick of Mom and thrilled to see you. Mom would then start bitching at you. It became a vicious cycle because she'd drive you further away. I guess I've been afraid that I will end up in a lousy marriage like yours and Mom's. I know Mom loved you, but you didn't show her much love. I don't recall you two ever kissing or hugging. I'm not passing judgment on you or Mom, or blaming anyone. No one's at fault, but I pray that my wife and I treat each other with more respect than you and Mom showed to each other. She bitched at you and you ignored her.

It's great to know that you and your second wife respect and love each other. It's wonderful to see. You're damn lucky and so is she.

I've always known that you loved me, but as a kid I didn't think that Mom loved me. Now I know that she did, always, but she was frustrated terribly because she got fat and you rejected her. She took it out on us kids, especially on me. I don't know whether you ever realized how your attitude toward Mom affected us directly. It's taken me years to realize it. It must have been tough on you to all of a sudden have two young boys and an over-weight, nagging wife. I probably would have reacted the same way as you did. I guess I'm mentioning all this because you and I have never talked about it and it's been bugging the hell out of me.

There's been a lot of positive things happen in our family too, and between you and me. You've coached my teams, lent me $, bailed me out of jail, and put your butt on the line for me more than once. I loved you for that and always will. I just want to be able to communicate with you on a deeper level. It's hard to do. I know your childhood was troubled. I can't imagine losing my father at age six, or whatever age, and then losing my mother in my early twenties. You don't talk about that much, and I'd like to know more about them. I don't even know where their graves are. I want to get to know more about my aunt—it didn't really dawn on me until recently that she could have been like a grandmother to us all these years.

Just trying to get rid of some emotional baggage here—it's no one's fault that I've been carrying it around, but it's my fault and loss if I don't deal with it now. So I'm trying to deal with it and I need your help to talk about it. I'm basically very happy with my life now, but I need to deal with the baggage so that I'm not emotionally harnessed anymore. And I don't want any roadblocks that prevent you and me from having a great relationship. Mom and I are working on it too.

The rest of the letter deals with the logistics of his upcoming visit home. During that visit, he and his father had many talks that put their relationship on a whole new plane. Often it's not so much the letters themselves as the conversations they make possible that move us forward.

David has spent years working on his issues in therapy. His work as an actor has been part of that process, and he has used his therapeutic discoveries to enhance and enrich his acting. The rigid mask that used to appear on his videotapes is gone, gradually replaced by a charming, playful, even mischievous person. Looking at his recent tapes, you might find it hard to believe that this is the same person who looked so shut down and empty a few years ago. About his new tapes, David says, "That's who I am. That's who I feel I am when I'm acting. It was never there before. It used to be a mask."

The Healing Power of Writing and Talking

Keeping emotional secrets, not allowing ourselves to heal old hurts, only keeps us stuck. Shame, guilt, and repression distance us from our creative center.

Recent studies at Southern Methodist and Ohio State universities show that people who write or talk about their feelings and internal problems have stronger immune systems, make fewer visits to the doctor, and seem happier than those who do not. Dr. Ann Ulanov, an analyst in private practice in New York City, favors this kind of "confession" because, as she said in an interview in *Newsday*, "keeping secrets isolates people, makes them guilty and ashamed. Traumatic events are generally repressed experiences. Talking about them is like finding a missing piece of the puzzle."

The various forms of writing discussed in this chapter can give us fuller access to the creative part of ourselves. Notes on the various aspects of our work, lists that keep us focused and moving forward, and letters to the past that release emotional baggage all reveal new dimensions and richer parts of ourselves, bringing new elements of magic to our journey.

chapter 5
Using Imagery and Ritual

Internal landscapes are the images that we see when we look inside ourselves. They create a picture of how our lives look to us. They come from the imagination, and they speak to us in the images of the right brain.

Internal landscapes reflect both our emotional state and the way we see ourselves and our world. They can tell us volumes about ourselves and about our creative work. When something is wrong, working with these images can help to pinpoint the problem, and may even suggest solutions.

Everyone's internal landscape looks different. One person might see dark, ominous clouds surrounding hostile craggy mountains. Another person might see a peaceful green meadow with fawns grazing contentedly at the edge of a rich, silent forest.

Most people's internal landscapes fall somewhere between these two extremes. There may be danger present—perhaps a mountain precipice to be scaled—but that dangerous image can also represent adventure, opportunity, and achievement. We are the best interpreters of our personal symbols. The exercises in this chapter will help us to identify those symbols.

The three imaging exercises that my clients have found most helpful are those I call "The Beach," "180 Degrees," and "The Dark Pond." These exercises are designed to:

- Open our eyes to our perception of what our lives are like now.
- Let us feel what our lives would be like if things were different.
- Enable us to start the process of change.
- Create a place to put emotional baggage that we don't need right now.

These exercises should be undertaken with care. It is important to create a safe, secure environment in which we won't be interrupted and to have enough time to move slowly back from each exercise into everyday life.

The exercises are not intended to be deep therapeutic experiences but rather to give hints about where problems and their solutions may lie. They focus on our feelings about what our lives are like, and they should not be subjected to strict or minute interpretation.

If we feel blocked and can't see a landscape, or if the landscape is frightening, it's best not to push ourselves. When an exercise becomes uncomfortable, we don't have to continue. It's better simply to stop and do something kind for ourselves. If the discomfort continues, we can call a friend, watch a favorite movie, go running or walking, or even call a therapist and make an appointment.

The Beach

There are five steps to this exercise:

1. Close your eyes and imagine that you are standing on a beach looking out over the ocean. Let the beach symbolize how your life feels now. How does it look? Can you see the ocean clearly? Are there all kinds of things in the way? Maybe it is empty, or full of half-finished things. Maybe it is calm and serene, the waves lapping gently on the shore. Is your beach cluttered? Desolate and windswept? You don't have to do anything about it, just feel what it is like to look at it and to walk along it. Take your time and look at whatever is there. What is the feeling it arouses in you?

2. As you look at your beach or walk along it, consider all the things you don't like having on that beach, all the negative elements. You don't have to identify what they represent right now. If you don't want them there, pick them up and put them off to the side on an imaginary table. You can even wrap them up if you want to. Take a good look at each of them, and also at the space that is left on the beach when each has been moved away.

3. Now turn back to the beach. How does it look and feel? More space? More breathing room? Can you see the horizon more clearly? Breathe deeply, relax a little, and just feel what it is like now. Let your shoulders relax. Look at the "stuff" you put on the table. If there is anything you feel you must change your mind about, unwrap it and put it back on the beach. Maybe there is a better place for it now. It's your beach. You can have it any way you want.

4. Look at the table and unwrap what is left. What does it all represent to you? The committee you agreed to serve on, against your desires and better judgment? You know what to do: Get off it. You will recognize every piece of clutter on the table. At this point, just be aware of what each piece represents. An item might be something as simple as not having read a script you promised your agent you'd read last week — in which case you just promise yourself that you'll read it by Thursday, and you call your agent to let her know you'll have it done by then. Or a piece of the clutter might represent something as major as confronting the fact that your marriage isn't working. What steps need to be taken to resolve this enormous intrusion on your beach and your work?

If there is a project that's been haunting you for years, but you never seem to get to it, try throwing it away. Are there other items that can be handled with a phone call? If you realize there's no way you're ever going to sit down and write a thank-you letter to Aunt Lucy for last year's birthday present, can you just pick up the phone, absorb the expense, and get that distracting item off your table?

Maybe one of your items is the fact that you didn't get that role last March, and you've been carrying that "failure" around for months. Can you let go of that so it won't get in the way of future opportunities?

Just taking the time and energy to put those unwanted items on the table and to examine them *starts the process of change.* You may choose not to do anything about some of the items at this point, but you have at least identified what the negative elements are and what you need to do to handle them. This exercise gives us a sense of how good it would feel to have only a few items left on the table. That in itself is productive: We have a picture in our minds of solving the problems, and all change begins as a picture in our minds. We've felt that solutions are possible and this sense of the possibilities will start the internal work.

5. Now back to the beach. Walk down it. What would you like to put in some of the space you've cleared? You are *not going to fill up your beach again,* so choose carefully. Would it be an afternoon each week to work with a scene partner? Time at least once a week to get out to the beach or to a museum or to whatever place pleases you, just to dream and wander and allow your imagination to be fed? How do these things feel?

Now there are some new things on the beach, and more space than there was before. Maybe it still needs some rearranging; go ahead and do that. In your mind's eye, your beach can look any way you want it to. Walk down it again and get a sense of how it feels. Does it feel now like a place where you can breathe easily and relax? If it feels more comfortable, take a few moments to savor it, and then leave the beach. Remember that you can return to your landscape, and to this feeling, whenever you wish.

The more we repeat this exercise, the more progress we make. The vision of examining all the items on the table will grow stronger each time, and so will the resolve to do something about them. Each time, the space on the beach that is available for creative work will increase.

Ellen: Living in a dangerous landscape

Ellen is a strong and successful actress. When I asked her to talk about her internal landscape, she described a beach with dangerous rocks and outcroppings around which the waves broke fiercely. She liked to walk on the beach, and part of her enjoyed the danger, while part of her was deeply afraid—afraid that she would jump off one of the rocks into the ocean and drown.

Ellen had felt for some time that she was trying to destroy herself, even in the midst of trying to be successful. She mentioned that it sometimes took all her energy to keep herself from jumping off the rocks. A part of her wanted to jump, while the rest wanted to be safe.

Ellen is now in therapy to work out the deeper issues behind her destructive impulses. Meanwhile, she has gradually changed her landscape into a safer one. First she moved the rocks to the ends of the beach, where she could examine them safely. She realized that some of the smaller rocks were left over from past errors in judgment, and she was able to get rid of them easily. The dangerous rocks still exist, but they are far away and much less threatening. Now she can walk down her beach without feeling the urge to jump.

180 Degrees

This is another exercise that opens our eyes to the fact that we can change our lives. It engages the image-forming right brain in the process of identifying and solving problems. It helps clarify what we are feeling about our lives and work, showing us exactly what the problems are and suggesting creative solutions that might not occur to the more analytical left side of the brain.

This exercise has four steps:

1. Paint a picture in your mind of what your life feels like right now. This can be a physical landscape—desert, mountains, beach, meadow, rolling plain—or some other type of image entirely. (One client, for example, saw herself in a large dirty house that she had to finish cleaning.) Let yourself experience and absorb the feelings that accompany this image.

2. Now turn slowly, with your eyes closed, 180 degrees from where you are looking, to see a picture of your life as you would like it to be. Start to walk toward that picture in your imagination. The image may change drastically from that formed in the first step, or it may reflect only minor differences. There may be blanks in this new painting, because it is still unfamiliar. Let yourself enter more deeply into this landscape and start filling in the blank spots. Feel what it would be like to act in this new environment.

3. Compare the two landscapes. Are there any similarities? What are the most striking differences?

4. See what steps you might take right now to start moving from the first landscape into the second. You may not feel like making a drastic move right away, but you can begin to consider opening up that new landscape to yourself and taking the first steps toward making it real.

Yvonne: Imagining a landscape of hope

Yvonne grew up in a small Oregon town and eventually moved to Los Angeles, where she did very well for a short time. She worked on a network show, and it looked as though a career were being handed to her on a silver platter. But Yvonne's internal landscape reflected something quite different.

She was very attractive, and felt that her beauty was the only reason she was succeeding. Between this perception and the stresses of living in a large city, her work became erratic. She was fired from the network show and ended up back home in Oregon doing a local television show once a week. She didn't like the town, and she didn't like what she was doing.

I asked Yvonne to paint a picture in words of how she saw the landscape of her life. She saw a desert, parched and dry, with some dead grass in small clumps here and there. The ground was cracked, and a paving-stone pattern stretched out almost as far as the eye could see.

Beyond the desert were mountains, dangerous mountains that she was afraid to approach. I asked her what the mountains represented, and she replied, "Los Angeles. It's dangerous for me to go there." The small town in Oregon might be as empty and desolate as the desert, but at least it wasn't as dangerous as Los Angeles.

"So you live in a desert with mountains on the other side of it, and the mountains are dangerous," I said. "Is this how you want to live?"

"No," she said, "but that's all there seems to be, desert or danger."

I suggested that she close her eyes, turn around 180 degrees from where she stood looking into the desert, and create another scene that represented her life as she would like it to be. She saw a green, grassy valley with a path leading through it to trees and softly rolling hills.

Yvonne's face changed as she imagined this new and inviting landscape. She smiled as she agreed to try walking into it and putting the desert behind her.

At the end of the exercise, Yvonne turned to me and said, "I had forgotten that there was any other way to be. Maybe I can get closer to what I want for my life." Letting herself experience that feeling, that hope, was the first in a series of steps. They were small steps at first: She committed time to exploring where she might work that was neither a desert nor a dangerous mountain to her. She looked seriously at how much time she wanted to devote to acting. She began taking better care of the child within her, and she ended a destructive relationship.

Creating an image of her internal landscape didn't make Yvonne's problems vanish, but it did give her a start. For the first time in many years, she got a look at something other than the desert, and she no longer felt trapped. Now she had a clear feeling that there were other possibilities, that there was hope, and that if she could imagine a new life, then maybe she could make it real.

Dan: Walking around danger

Internal landscapes are wonderful for showing us whether we need to ease up on ourselves. In Dan's first internal landscape, he was clinging by perilous footholds and handholds to the side of a rugged mountain, with angry winds and dark clouds swirling all around him. He felt that if he moved one hand, he might fall off—and yet he needed to get to the top of the mountain.

When I asked him what was up there, he said, "I think another mountain, even more dangerous."

We talked about the mountain and why he chose to stay in that perilous position. Eventually he admitted that he really would like to come down off the mountain and find another path for his life.

Dan had been a successful child actor at the age of five, and had continued to work on stage and in film through his teens. But when he reached his midtwenties, there were fewer and fewer roles for him.. He simply wasn't getting cast. Acting was no longer very important to him, and he wasn't at all sure he wanted to keep doing it, but he still wanted to do something creative. He had made such a commitment to acting that it was hard to abandon his investment of time and energy. He was also afraid of what family, friends, and people in the industry would say if he decided to give up the struggle.

Dan agreed to imagine what it would be like if he came slowly down from the side of the rugged mountain. When he was at the bottom, he turned to his right and saw a gently sloping path winding around the foot of the mountain. He felt that it would be a lot more comfortable to walk on that path and see where it led him.

The differences between Dan's present internal landscape and his ideal one were striking. He had *thought* about the fact that he wasn't happy, but he had never *felt* so viscerally what was happening to his life.

He told me later that for nearly a week after doing this exercise he walked around in a daze, unable to believe that he had been living in such peril without really being aware of it.

When I asked him what appealed to him as a career other than acting, Dan said that he had always wanted to work with children. He decided to take a summer off and work as a drama teacher at a children's camp. He called his agent and said that he was taking some time off and would call when he got back to town in the fall.

When he came back, he told his agent, friends, and family that his summer's work with children had been the most rewarding of his life and that, for now, it was what he wanted to do. No one had anything but good feelings about his change of career. Several people, including his agent, had felt for some time that things were not going well for him. Walking on the path around the foot of the mountain is working much better for Dan than scaling a precipice. Someday he may decide to return to acting professionally, but not if it makes him feel that he is in danger.

Kay: Living behind glass

Kay felt as if she were living inside a large glass prism. She could see out and people could see in, but they couldn't hear her. However, she could hear them. She described it as "my beautiful, carefully built prism. It's beautiful in here, but I can't get out."

Kay had built a perfectly constructed life without apparent flaws. It all looked wonderful from the outside; it even looked as if she were doing everything she wanted to do. But in reality, she had built a prison. The essence of who she was couldn't be heard, nor could she reach out to people. She could just make little gestures from inside her prison.

Her husband and mother seemed supportive, and apparently had no problems with her acting career. But when pressed, Kay admitted that she got mixed messages from them. They said that acting was okay, but every time she went out of town on a shoot and was gone for a few weeks, they seemed resentful and accusatory. Her mother talked a great deal about children and about being a grandmother. Kay felt as though she were still being treated as a child.

She agreed that she was partly responsible for the situation continuing; after all, she was the one who kept saying that it was all perfect.

I asked Kay whether her prism had a door. She looked surprised and said she didn't know.

"Have you ever turned around and faced the other way?" I asked.

"No, I'm on show. I have to look right. I can't turn my back. I have to behave the way they want me to—I have to do the right thing."

"How do you know what 'right' is?"

"Everyone is looking at me through a different facet of the prism, and that tells me how to behave."

"But if you could turn around 180 degrees, would there be a door behind you?"

"I think there is a door because my mother and my husband are sometimes in the prism with me."

The prism did have a door; it was behind her and easy to open. Kay walked through it toward a lake with foothills sloping up to high snow-capped mountains. The trees, which were turning color, were filled with birds, and there were paths along the shore of the lake to explore. It was a landscape of freedom where she could wander the paths, come home safely, and wander out again. Her husband and mother were happy to see her go down these paths and happy to see her return. The experience moved her in ways that no intellectual understanding of her situation could have.

There followed months of hard work in therapy to change the structure of Kay's family so that she could speak openly about her needs. She learned that people could hear her when she spoke clearly, and was able to set up new ground rules about how her work and her family's needs could be integrated.

Feeling what it would be like to be out of the prism was the first step. Until she described the prism in this exercise, and saw how much it isolated her, Kay had not been fully aware of what was happening in her life.

★ ★ ★

Some people actually paint or draw their "before" and "after" internal landscapes. This is a different kind of process. People who are more visual often discover things in their paintings that they might have missed in verbal or written descriptions.

By turning around 180 degrees and repainting our internal landscape, we can look at ways to make both our personal life and our creative work more productive and satisfying. This exercise sparks the realization that things don't have to be the way they are now. If we can imagine different surroundings, we can begin the journey toward them. This imaginary scouting mission makes it easier to embark on the actual journey toward change.

The Dark Pond

The dark pond is an imaginary place where we can leave all our fears, tears, sorrow, anger, and other negative emotions. It is also a place where we can go later to examine and understand those same feelings in safety, without letting them take over our lives.

Each of us can design our own pond. This is how my client Rhonda described hers:

> My pond is nestled at the base of foothills, with higher mountains behind them. Some of the higher mountains have snow on them. The lower levels are covered with shrubs and tall red-woods. Around the pond itself there are more trees, except on the side from which I view it. From where I stand, a grassy bank slopes gently down to the water.
>
> Toward the far side of the pond are aspens that turn gold in the fall, and closer to me are two tall maples that turn scarlet when the aspens lose their leaves. Under these trees, smaller shrubs and bushes flourish.
>
> The water in the pond does not reflect any light or images; it is dark. There is not a "No Swimming" sign posted, but there might as well be. I can neither swim nor drown in the pond.

No matter how many tears or how much grief or anger we take to the pond, it will always hold what we leave. Later, if we want, we can come back to consider these feelings and try to solve the problems. Whatever we need from the pond will be available. For rehearsals, readings, and performances, we can take just enough tears, just enough anger, just enough guilt for the role so that we don't feel overwhelmed by emotion when we are working. Having a place to put these feelings frees us to use them in acting. We can decide which emotions to take with us and use as tools and which to simply let sink to the bottom and dissolve.

My clients have been extremely creative in their use of the dark pond. Most use it in their personal lives as well as in their work.

John stops at his dark pond after a rehearsal or shoot. He leaves there all the problems and frustrations that have built up during the day or week so that he doesn't take them home to his wife and children. He spends a little time at the pond understanding and defining the shape and dimensions of these problems, and then he lets them go.

Sometimes he takes some time during the weekend to return to the dark pond to try to solve some of those problems, but he doesn't bring them to the dinner table with him. He walks into his home "clean," and he feels that the quality of his family life has improved immensely since he has been visiting the dark pond. He keeps his home life separate from his professional life, and he can approach each new project without emotional baggage from the last one.

Dick uses his dark pond in a slightly different way. He makes quick visits many times during the day, leaving whatever is bothering him at the moment so that he can concentrate on what he is doing, and then returning later to sort it all out.

When Dick really needs to focus on what is going on in the moment, he can't afford to be distracted. If something is bothering him on a film set, for instance, he will make a quick stop at the pond to dump his anger, and then go back later to work on it when he has more time and energy.

He may even be able to take some of that anger to another role, where it is appropriate. Or he may take a safe amount of it back to the person who made him angry and let him or her know how he felt, then throw the whole thing back into the pond. This process lets Dick work "clean"; what is going on around him doesn't affect the quality of his work.

The dark pond exercise is different from therapy, where clients are often asked to work through their emotions rather than simply let them go. In the dark pond, we just release them temporarily so that we can get on with our work unhindered. Often the relief of laying down these burdens is so great that people will find a way to work through them later in order to let them go for good.

The Laughter Pond

Some of my clients have invented a second pond, a pond of laughter, fun, and delight. They don't dump in it; they come to it to take what they need for a rehearsal or performance. One actress has her "bright pond" positioned just behind her when she is looking into the dark pond so that, when she turns away from the dark pond, she can see the bright one. She doesn't always go to it, but she knows that it's there.

Symbols are important; they are part of the language of the right brain. The landscapes we see in our imagination have tremendous power. They can guide us out of stifling circumstances and lead us into the light. The realization that our lives can be different, and the visceral experience of what that new reality feels like, mark the beginnings of change.

The Importance of Ritual

In each of these imagery exercises, ritual plays an important part. Taking the time to be quiet and alone, looking inside and allowing our internal landscapes to emerge, exploring these images — all of these activities can become personal rituals that lead to a sense of peace and confidence.

Ritual — the simple repetition of a phrase or activity that we have endowed with meaning — can become a powerful ally in our work as actors. Perhaps we find a talisman that we can carry with us to satisfy the need of the child within for a comforting object; or perhaps we simply take the time to breathe deeply and say something like "I am going to do good work" before each interview or audition. We might make a ritual out of the process of dressing and preparing for work, out of collecting everything we need to take with us, or out of warming up and putting on makeup before a performance. When we treat these simple acts as rituals, they help us to feel grounded and available before we launch ourselves into creative work.

part three

The Nuts and Bolts: Practical Applications

chapter 6
Staying Sane in a Crazy World

When we begin working on our own blocks — perhaps discovering some uncomfortable things about ourselves, learning to transform and forgive the past, and moving into new relationships with ourselves, with the people in our lives, and with our acting — sometimes we unconsciously assume that the rest of the world is doing the same thing. We assume, or maybe just hope, that others in our industry have also been dissolving barriers, finding new vistas of creativity, and discovering a new wholeness within themselves.

Then we go to a rehearsal, meet with our agent, or audition for a role and realize that these assumptions aren't entirely accurate. The industry is actually pretty much the same as it was when we last looked. People haven't made a wholesale renunciation of ego in favor of generosity and support. Creative expression has not replaced profit as the bottom line. Many people are still acting as if they were in the midst of their dysfunctional families — only now they hold a lot of power in the industry and in our lives. In fact, on our darker days, the whole industry can look like one big dysfunctional family. The fact that we are working hard on ourselves while others continue in their old patterns hardly seems fair; but then, no one promised us that life would be fair.

What saves us is remembering that we are not doing this healing work for anybody else, or so that anybody else will do it too. We're doing it for ourselves. If it moves us closer to our creative center, that's all that matters. The rest of the world is under no obligation to do this work; they simply won't reap the same benefits as we do.

Dysfunction does not discriminate. Studio heads, production staff, directors, and casting directors are not immune. The advantage we have is that, having done some of this work on ourselves, we're more likely to recognize dysfunctional behavior when we see it in others.

Our challenge will be to avoid becoming a part of the dysfunctional drama. If we recognize what is happening, we can say to the vulnerable child within who was hurt in this situation before, "Look out. Don't get trapped. Let me handle this." Then we can manage the situation in an adult way, in a way that allows us to do our work and do it well. There is no need for us to be taken hostage again at this point in life. We don't have to keep on playing old games.

Recognizing Dysfunctional Behavior

The following list is a reminder of the behaviors that can result from dysfunctional backgrounds. It is based on material distributed by Adult Children of Alcoholics, and is written from the point of view of those of us who have survived a dysfunctional upbringing:

- We become isolated and afraid of other people, especially authority figures.
- We are frightened by anger and personal criticism.
- We don't act; we react.
- We live life from the viewpoint of victims and are attracted to victims or rescuers in our love, friendship, and career relationships.
- We feel responsible for our unstable families and, in the present, feel ineligible to live independently.

- We feel guilty when we stand up for ourselves instead of giving in to others.
- We are approval seekers, and we tend to lose our identities in the process of looking for approval.
- We have an overdeveloped sense of responsibility toward others, but rarely consider our responsibility to ourselves.

Strongly abusive situations usually produce extreme versions of these traits; mildly abusive situations produce less extreme versions. In any case, keeping this list in mind during interactions with people who hold power over us in the industry can alert us to potential problems.

In an interview for the *Tarrytown Newsletter*, Harry Levinson, a psychologist at Harvard Medical School, stated that "management may play the role of overbearing parents or may carelessly abandon their subordinates. Yet their hidden psychological agendas are the great cause of inefficiency and disaffection on the job. . . . These old [from the past] psychological contracts can make the workplace a hotbed of guilt, rivalry, and dependence."

Levinson adds, "Though we live in a psychological age, business leaders are criminally unaware of feelings."

Those in power can sabotage our work in another, more subtle way. Westin Agor, director of the Public Administration Department at the University of Texas in El Paso and author of *Intuitive Management,* offers insight into this management pitfall: "To date, American management has followed the culture, emphasizing left-brain analytical thinking, and allowed the right brain, which is associated with emotional and more creative thinking, to atrophy. . . . Intuitive people are good at coming up with new ideas, but left-brained people tend to say these ideas are dumb, and then they end up fighting with each other. In that atmosphere, new ideas wither on the vine."

Producers, directors, and casting directors who share this left-brain emphasis may bring up our old feelings of being "different" or "wrong." If we are alert to this potential conflict, we won't let their criticism trigger us into abandoning our unique identity or shutting down the ideas that flow from our creative center.

Dealing with Power Plays

The dysfunctional family is a hierarchy of power, and so is the entertainment industry. Wherever there is a hierarchy of power, there will be similarities to the dysfunctional family. The system in the film and television industry is complex, but basically studios and networks hire producers, who hire directors and casting directors, who hire actors. In the theater, there may be a complicated structure at the top involving investors and producers, but again the producers hire a director, and together they hire actors. We can use this hierarchical structure to work through our blocks and get on with our work, or we can let it bring out the worst in everyone.

When directors, casting directors, and others who have power in the industry are unconsciously acting out dysfunctional family situations, they often try to draw us into their personal drama and force us into roles that can be devastating to a career. This is usually not deliberate—for the most part, they are unaware of what they are doing—but it is destructive nevertheless.

If these people felt that they were victims or hostages of power in their own families when they were growing up, then when they get into positions of power themselves, they will use power in the same way it was used on them. They will try to create victims and take hostages.

My client Reva had been at a new acting school only two weeks when she realized that the teacher, a man in his early fifties, was being emotionally abusive to her and coming on to her at the same time—just as her father had done. Maybe he was acting out something from his own emotional past, but that didn't make the situation any more comfortable for her. Their histories were a perfect match; the situation was guaranteed to trigger past patterns of behavior in both of them.

Reva, who had done a year of work with Adult Children of Alcoholics, recognized clearly what was happening. She decided not to get caught up in old games.

Reva went to the registrar and asked to transfer to a different class. She even said that some old stuff in her life was being triggered by the class she was in. She was told that she could not change class until the semester break, but she insisted and finally got her way. She approached the problem as a responsible adult and solved it—a minor victory, perhaps, but a significant one for her. Her old method would have been to say, "See, everything I do, I'm victimized. I guess that's what I get in this world. I guess I deserve it." But she was no longer willing to be a victim.

Working with Agents and Directors in a Healthy Way

The relationship between agent and actor can be particularly vulnerable to power plays because our professional success is so interdependent. Agents are perceived to have a great deal of power over their clients. Their job is to guide and counsel their clients and to help them get work. Although many agents are deeply concerned about their clients' well-being and foster independent, healthy relationships, others seem determined to make their clients feel dependent and endangered if they don't play the role of victim.

When actors who have survived a dysfunctional home have this type of agent, they find themselves in a diabolical match. Client and agent at first appear to get along well—after all, they both have a lot of experience in similar relationships—but ultimately the association will be counterproductive, especially for the actor.

Similarly, some directors and casting directors will go to the ends of the earth for actors. They create supportive environments, enabling actors to give daring and inspired performances. But others try to draw actors into their own personal drama.

There is always a temptation to abuse power, and a casting director has a great deal of power. When we are reading for a role, the casting director may get up and look out the window, fiddle with something on the desk, eat lunch, or even read another script. It's natural to be outraged by this kind of behavior, especially if we haven't taken the time to center and prepare ourselves for the possibility that some of our old buttons may be pushed.

On the other hand, it may be that the casting director was looking away simply to concentrate on our vocal quality or for some other equally valid reason. It may not be rudeness at all, and it probably isn't personal. Again, we have to be on the lookout for how another person's behavior can trigger something from our past. The director who is eating lunch while listening to us read is *not* the parent who never gave us enough attention. He or she is either simply a very busy or a very rude person with his or her own "stuff" that has nothing to do with us — unless we let it. If we fall into the trap and don't read well as a result, it's our problem, not the director's.

We no longer have to react to such situations in the way that our hurt, frightened child might have. We don't have to shut down our feelings, disconnect from our creative center, or retreat into our left brain. The only one we will hurt by doing those things is ourself. We have to make an effort to stay focused on what we want, which is the role, and to keep moving toward it.

Fighting for Change

The motion picture and theater worlds used to place a high premium on creative and imaginative people, people who never allowed their vision to be limited by what they already knew or by how much money they could make. These people understood, respected, and were excited by the process of discovering and venturing into the unknown.

Artists need to be able to experiment, to make mistakes, and to discover what works and what doesn't work. In repertory theater, it is still possible to do an esoteric, specialized, or experimental production because the financial success or failure of that one production does not determine whether the whole season or the theater itself is a success or failure. In film, however, this willingness to let artists experiment is extremely rare today. Some producers are wise enough to realize that experimentation is a good investment in the future of our craft, because it is how our new writers, directors, producers, and actors emerge — but these producers are the exception rather than the rule. Usually, the bottom line on the financial statement is the most important consideration.

This "bottom-line" perspective affects not only actors but also directors and individual producers who have vision and ideas. It affects casting directors and producers in a profound way. Their decisions for the most part must be safe and "bankable."

David Mamet's *Writing in Restaurants* (Viking, 1986) includes a piece titled "An Unhappy Family." Every creative artist should read it. The piece ends, "This unreasoned hierarchy of actor-director-producer has drained the theater of its most powerful force: the phenomenal strength and generosity of the actor; and, as in any situation of unhappy tyranny, the oppressed must free the oppressor."

When actors are treated with dignity and with respect for their skills and intuition, the revolution will be complete. But it is not likely that the "oppressors" will simply abandon their dysfunctional behavior without being urged to do so and without our example. Example, communication, and a respect for ourselves that prevents us from getting pulled into dysfunctional dramas are our most effective tools.

If the people who wield power in our industry were to release themselves and those who work with them (not *under* them) from the power hierarchy in order to join forces creatively, then we would be able to work together, not in power-oriented, destructive relationships, but as strong, independent, productive team members who respect one another. To bring about such change, we as actors can take the lead through our commitment to living a dignified and generous life. When one link in the chain has such strength and integrity, it is bound to have an effect on the links to which it is connected.

chapter 7
The Art of the Interview

"So, tell me something about yourself." This is how casting directors, agents, producers, directors, and others who appear to guard the gate that leads to our work often begin an interview. To me, these words are like the Chinese character that stands for both "danger" and "opportunity."

Danger and Opportunity

In my work as a casting director and agent, I was always amazed that people expressed surprise or panic when I said, "So, tell me something about yourself." It was the most predictable question in the world. They knew it would be asked, but it was often so intimidating that they seemed to draw a complete blank.

This question is dangerous because the answer reveals so much. But it presents an opportunity for exactly the same reason. How this question strikes us depends on whether we know who we are, feel comfortable with that person, and intend to be open and honest—or whether we're not sure exactly what we have inside, but we think it might be something bad, so we hope to conceal it and pretend to be the person we think the casting director wants us to be. The fact is that the truth usually bleeds through in any case, and we're better off not mixing messages by pretending to be someone we're not.

The interview is a business meeting, but it is also very personal. It's our best opportunity to let the casting director know who we are. Instead, we sometimes spend it looking up fearfully at the ceiling, clearing our throats, coughing, muttering, or otherwise acting as if we've been asked to talk about something we know nothing about.

Sometimes responses to "So, tell me something about yourself" are completely inappropriate. One casting director told me that when he asked an actor this question, he got the answer, "Well, I'm a waiter at [he named a well-known San Francisco restaurant]." The casting director asked about the restaurant's food, and they had a lively discussion about the chef and the quality of the menu. The actor left feeling that he had a new friend, and he did. Whenever the casting director goes to San Francisco, he calls up this actor and asks him for restaurant advice. He has never once hired him for a role in any of the films he has cast.

In some ways, the interview represents everything that is frightening about being a creative person. It demands a great deal of self-revelation, it requires that we be present in the moment and respond to changing circumstances, and it reminds us that we have to sell ourselves over and over again in ways that people with "regular" jobs never have to do.

In most other professions, a successful job interview yields long-term employment. Only in interviews for a television series, soap opera, or repertory season can this happen in the actor's world. Often an actor has to go on several interviews a day to secure the next job. Many interviews provide the opportunity for many rejections. Some people estimate that only one in every thirty-two interviews produces work.

The creative life often seems like one long interview. As soon as one role or project is over, we start from scratch with the next and have to get hired all over again. This condition doesn't change, regardless of how successful or well known we become. Even actors whose names are household words say that after each role they're afraid they'll never work again. They know that this isn't a rational assessment, but the feeling is real and the anxiety is profound.

Income aside, most of us simply feel better when we're working. The threat of not working can be terrifying, and it often looks as if the interviewer holds our future in his or her hands.

The interview demands everything we have, as artists and as people. We need to prepare for it, to bring to it every resource at our disposal. The rest of this chapter describes how to prepare for the interview. It also provides a glimpse of how directors look at our interviews.

Who Do They Want Me to Be?

The first few seconds of the interview are important both for us and for the interviewer. We are trying to make an impression, and the casting director is trying to see who we are. It feels as if he or she has us under a microscope, but actually we're in it together. The casting director has a job to do too; he or she has to find the best people for the parts being cast.

The casting director introduces himself or herself, takes our picture and résumé, settles back, and says, "So, tell me something about yourself."

This is the moment of truth. Does this person become for us a figure from the past—a teacher, a coach, an abusive parent—whose very presence makes fear well up and causes us to behave like the frightened child or the rebellious teenager? Or does he or she remain simply a person who is doing a job and looking for people who do just what we do?

Casting directors lead extraordinarily busy and pressured lives. They conduct complicated negotiations all day long, and they have to make many hard decisions every day.

One of my clients, Ben, was a promising young actor who didn't have a great deal of experience. His agent had spoken about him in glowing terms to the casting director for a film, and the casting director was hoping against hope that the search would end with him. But Ben seemed so ill at ease that it was difficult to get a fix on who he was. He read well, but the casting director still had an uneasy feeling and couldn't make up his mind whether to have the film's director meet him. Since this director conducted difficult interviews and the casting director was not sure whether Ben could relax enough to be himself, he didn't get a chance to read for the role.

I once held a workshop in Berkeley for student actors, and one of the exercises was to have them interview with a casting director, played by me. I noticed, as did the rest of the class, that several of the students seemed overtly or covertly angry with me as the casting director. When I asked them about this, they replied:

- "I don't like it that you have the power to get me work, and if you don't like me, you won't do that."
- "I'm angry at you because I don't know what the right thing to say is, and I know I must say the right thing."
- "This is important and I don't feel ready for it."
- "I'm not angry. What makes you say that?"

When I probed further, I got responses like these:

- "My brother is an engineer earning $40,000 a year, and I have to go out and make people like you like me. I'm not making any money at all and he's younger than I am."
- "You remind me of my mother, and she has never approved of my being an actor. I'm angry that you remind me of her, but that's only part of it. I'm angry because I know I should get you to like me. Instead, I really want to say all the things to you that I never said to my mother."

These are the kinds of issues we want to clear up *before* the interview with the casting director. He or she wants to see *us,* not our fears from the past.

If there is a possibility that these fears may surface, we can have a talk with our child before the interview, trying to anticipate what might happen and how the child might react. If our child has a particular fear of authority figures, we can talk with him or her about the fact that this is simply a casting director who wants to cast a film, and not the person from the past who prompts such fear.

HERE NOW!

We don't want our child to curl up into a fetal position in the middle of the interview, petrified of saying or doing anything. Nor do we want the child acting out like an angry teenager who is just trying to cover up the fear and hurt. An interview with a casting director is *not* the place to go back and relive old incidents.

When people ask me, "Who should I be in this interview?" I always answer, "Yourself." The interview is the time to let the casting director know who we are. There will be plenty of time later, when we read, to create a character and show our acting skill. Then we can be as opinionated, mean, funny, or stupid as the role demands. The casting director won't invest us with those qualities; he or she will just see how skilled we are at our craft.

It's fine to let a casting director know if we have certain skills that make us especially suitable for a particular role, but these are secondary to who we are and to our acting skills. If we're interviewing for the part of a cowboy, for instance, we can let the casting director know such relevant information as the fact that we grew up in Montana and practically lived on horseback.

We're at this interview because we are actors; our skill is not in question. The only question is: How right are we for this role? The casting director wouldn't have seen us without a reason. Either our agent convinced him or her that we might be right for the role, or the casting director has seen us and liked our work, or he or she is willing to cast an "unknown."

It's almost always a mistake to go into an interview playing what we imagine the role to be, or to try to second-guess what a casting director wants us to say or do. He or she does not want to see us as the manic killer, the depressed convict, or whatever the role is. Casting directors first want to see *us;* then they want to see us play the role. Our job is to be secure enough to be vulnerable, to let them see us as we are.

This also lets a casting director keep other options open. He or she may not want us for the role we came in to read for, but perhaps we'd be perfect for another. The casting director might say, "You know, I asked you to come in for the role of Peter, but I think you might be more interesting as Joseph. Take a look at these scenes and come back this afternoon."

When I am working as a casting director and I see an actor come through my door, I need to be free to see simply him. I may be thinking, "Hmm, interesting . . . Great look for the younger brother, even has the same eyes . . . There's a sweetness there . . . Maybe, if he can act, he's a good possibility."

I introduce myself, and so does he. He doesn't look at ease. Of course he doesn't. He thinks he's being judged, but what I'm thinking is, "Great, he can look really ill at ease and vulnerable. Wonder what he'll do with anger. I bet he can play the early scenes without even trying. I'll get him to read that big angry scene and see what happens."

He has already succeeded at much of the interview without doing anything other than be himself and be natural. If he can fight through his natural sweetness and vulnerability to express real anger, then I will have no question about having the director hear him read. That is, after all, what we both want out of this interview.

I could not have made that decision if the actor had come into the office projecting a self-assured, totally secure presence and had not allowed me to see who he really was. I might have suspected that there was someone underneath who *could* do the role, but, even assuming I had the time to unearth that person, how could I know whether he would stay unearthed in rehearsal or on the set? And would the director take the time to keep him unearthed in every take?

Casting directors don't have the time to do this unearthing, and it's not their job to do it. The work that enables us simply to *be* is work that we must do ourselves. We bring the result of that work to interviews, auditions, rehearsals, and performances.

Selling ourselves in a role prevents us from *being* ourselves. The key is to relax the mind and body, so that both attitude and body language communicate that we are comfortable with ourselves.

Many interviews are done on tape. Many of us hate videotape, but it is a wonderful tool and one that every actor would do well to master. We may have to work with it daily until we become completely comfortable with it. The excuse that we didn't do well because the audition was on tape is no longer acceptable.

Exactly the same principles apply to an audition on tape as to an audition in person, but we have even less time to accomplish the same results. We first identify ourselves by name and (if asked) give the name of the agency that represents us. The way we say our name reveals a great deal about how we feel about ourselves and our talent. If we say it in a way that questions our very existence, we will never get cast. Actors who sound as if they can't believe anyone would want them, or as if they wish people would do them a favor and cast them even though they don't deserve it, or as if they're mad at everyone in the industry because they haven't been cast enough, aren't going to get a lot of parts.

The kind of work described in Part Two of this book can help us feel secure enough in ourselves and our skills to reveal to the casting director who we really are. Since interviews and auditions are here to stay, this work will prove well worth the effort.

Speaking a Résumé

We think of résumés as career summaries that are written down, and we do give this printed version to the casting director, along with a photograph. But almost always, part of the interview also involves our giving a spoken version of that same résumé. For example, the casting director may ask questions about where we have worked, what we are rehearsing, or what classes and work-shops we have taken, simply as a way of making conversation. He or she wants to get to know us better, and the business of acting is, after all, what we have in common. Or the casting director may say something like, "What have you been up to lately?"

Our delivery of this spoken résumé should emerge naturally from who we are, rather than sounding like something we have memorized. The passion, vitality, and interest with which we describe our work need to be as great as the energy that goes into doing the work itself.

We should never apologize for what we have done, or belittle a role we have played. Such apologies sound as if we don't respect ourselves, our work, or certain parts of the industry. We have chosen to do the work we have done, and these roles have brought us to where we are today. We should be in love with all of it.

If the résumé is slender, there's nothing wrong with saying so. The casting director knows it already. What he or she is looking for is the passion, the commitment, and the unique qualities that we can bring to a role, not a long list of credits. If we try to be someone we are not, we may destroy our chances of being cast.

It's important to keep our verbal résumé updated. We can mention new work and edit out some of the older, less significant jobs. The résumé — verbal or written — is a tool of the trade; it should be kept sharp.

Learning to Listen

After the verbal résumé, the casting director usually asks some questions. *Listening to these questions is crucial.* If we go into the interview with a hidden agenda, with certain things we are going to say no matter what we are asked, we won't be able to listen to the questions and respond authentically. The casting director may be asking those questions just to see how we listen, or to see what we look like when we're thinking.

We may be asked to read a role differently from the way we've conceived it. I've heard many actors say, after a reading, "I thought it would be completely different. It really threw me when she asked me to do it that way. I was all ready to do it the other way, how *I* saw it."

It's dangerous to go into an interview expecting to play a scene as a set piece. We must always be able to adjust and operate in the moment. This is easy to do if we are being ourselves, impossible if we are already playing a role.

The audition process doesn't end when the interview is over; keeping in mind what happens next can help us be ourselves. The casting director will make recommendations to the director. If we have made it difficult for the casting director to see who we are, or to get a fix on us, he or she may say to the director, "I'm not sure. I think there is something interesting here, but I haven't been able to get at it."

Such an assessment puts us in a difficult position if we do get a chance to meet the director. We can't be sure we're what she wants, she's not sure who we are, and no one is altogether sure what anyone else is doing there. This is not usually a good beginning, and is not likely to reach that happy conclusion in which the director finds an interesting actor and the actor gets the role.

After we're established in the profession, the interview procedure is not so intimidating. Casting directors have an enormous capacity for remembering actors, and they take notes on everyone who reads for them. Well-established actors usually have to read only for the director or producer, not the casting director. But of course, the first question the director or producer asks will be, "So, tell me something about yourself." We always have to start from square one.

As we become even more successful, the casting director and director will make their decision based on work we've already done. Even then, they will call our agent at some point and ask that we "have lunch" or "come over and meet" with them "just so we can get to know each other better."

No matter how experienced or famous we become, most of us wonder before every interview, "What the hell do they want to see?" The answer will always be: They want to see _us_.

What the Casting Director Sees

Perhaps some of the notes I took while working as a casting director will help clarify the casting director's process. Each number represents a different actor. There were about thirty roles to fill, and these notes come from just a portion of one session.

1. Could be the doctor . . . maybe . . . but he is a little indirect. Perhaps callback . . . maybe.
2. Eager to please — like a puppy.
3. Wonderful as always . . . good good actor . . . could he look 50?
4. Interesting . . . dark side . . . nice smile . . . maybe.

5. Ummm . . . no.
6. Surprised me — she's really improved . . . nice.
7. Tried too hard . . . wouldn't calm down.
8. Great mother . . . really understands the role . . . like she's been there.
9. Sends telegrams — no.
10. Didn't believe his work — no.
11. Odd and crazy but interesting — try to get K (the director) to read him.
12. Too commercial, not real.
13. Vulnerable, great pregnant teenager . . . look as is in callback.
14. Maybe for Valerie if he wants it soft . . . not sure.
15. Probably too good-looking but he's a good actor . . . maybe.
16. He's got the anger . . . can he control it? Good reading.
17. Maybe . . . No — doesn't take direction.
18. Interviews badly . . . acts like an angel . . . Yes — talk with him before K sees him.
19. Nice nice actress . . . there must be something for her . . . what?
20. Dammit, looks too old now.

And so on through days of interviewing. From this group of twenty actors, six were called back to read for the director.

Understanding what the casting director sees can teach us a great deal about ourselves, as well as help us to master the art of interviewing.

Scott: Spinning webs of words

Scott is a twenty-five-year-old actor living in California. He came to see me because he thought he might be in the wrong profession. He didn't feel as anguished about himself or his life as other actors seemed to be, and he thought that either there was something wrong with him or that he wasn't really meant to be an actor after all because he wasn't miserable. He just loved the feelings that acting produced, and he wanted to get on with it in the simplest and most direct way.

My first question to him was, "So, tell me about yourself." He responded by talking a mile a minute about the universe, life, goodness, truth, the universe again. The more he talked, the more he got into his head and away from his body and his feelings, and the more vocally restricted he became. I soon lost track of what he was saying, unable to get any sense of who he was.

I asked him to slow down, to focus on where he was and what we were doing, and on the fact that we were there to talk about him as an actor. I pointed out that I had asked him to tell me something about himself, and that he hadn't done that at all.

If I had been a casting director during that interview, I wouldn't have had any idea who Scott was, except that he was on some kind of head trip that I didn't care to go on with him. My job as a casting director would have been to get a sense of him as an actor, and that would have been impossible through the fog of his words. I couldn't get even a glimpse of who he was.

During the rest of our time together that day, I learned that Scott had come from a very happy, athletic, and intellectual family. His father was a doctor, his mother a teacher. There were three other boys, all of whom had done very well athletically, and the family had played all kinds of sports together. The people in his family had always connected with one another either through the intellect or through athletics. And, although sports had been important, most of the praise had been for the intellect, and communication had usually taken an intellectual turn.

Scott had walked into our interview and had decided right away that we probably had little in common as athletes, so he had gone for intellectual approval, jumping into complex theories about the universe, love, life, beauty, and truth. Scott understood that it was easy for him to move away from his feelings by talking about what he *thought*. He knew that he was out of touch with his feelings, but he didn't seem to know what to do about it. He had come to me because he didn't think he was having the *right* feelings.

Since he didn't have the problems that other actors seemed to have, he had invented the "problem" of not having problems in an attempt to fit in. It was a great relief to learn that he was not deficient because he wasn't anguished, and that he no longer needed to invent things to worry about so that he'd be more like other actors — or, rather, more like his perception of other actors.

The first step for Scott in getting in touch with his feelings was to realize that whatever he felt was okay, even if he felt good! An interesting thing happened to his face when he realized this. While he had been talking from his head, he'd had a rather charming half-smile on his face. But when he began to respond from his feelings, a sparkling smile opened up on both sides of his mouth.

Scott said he was aware that when he was talking to someone new, he felt ill at ease and wanted to win their approval. That's when he would talk from his head, and that half-smile would appear on his face. It was almost as if the smile could go either way. If the new person did approve, he could open it up. If he or she didn't, he could close it down. Until Scott found out where he stood, he could hedge his bets.

He said he knew that he had blown many interviews with casting directors because he had tried to appear as he thought a good actor should appear — tortured and riddled with anxiety — only he didn't really know how to do that. This wasn't who he was. Because he didn't feel adequately anguished, he would jump into his intellect as the next best thing and would do to casting directors what he had done to me in the first part of our meeting.

Scott is funny, witty, healthy, and blessed with a delightful smile and considerable talent as an actor. When he can let casting directors see that person, he will get a lot of parts.

To meet the challenge of staying with his feelings more, Scott has started a personal journal in which he only writes about what he feels, not what he thinks. He is also taking meditation classes, and he talks frequently with his child. He has to be careful with that little boy, however, because the child is inclined to talk about what he thinks, rather than what he feels. Scott has to make it safe for him to talk about his feelings, and to give him a lot of approval for it. If Scott can stay grounded and connected to himself, he will be a very successful actor.

Ricardo: Acting as a caretaker

Sometimes an important event, such as a meeting with a casting director, can act as a catalyst, bringing up issues that have been dormant.

Ricardo grew up in New York and now lives on the West Coast. He is very charming and good-looking. He has a great time at interviews, and so do the casting directors, but he is seldom asked to read for parts. He always has wonderful things to say about the people who interview him, and casting directors say, "Oh, yeah, Ricardo. He's a great guy." Although Ricardo is an excellent actor, they rarely say, "Yes, I like his work."

In our first session together, I asked Ricardo, "So, why are we here?" Instead of answering me, he asked me what it was like to see people in ninety-minute sessions all day long. He asked if I enjoyed it, who looked after my emotional needs, and if I didn't find it draining. For a while I responded to his interest and concern, then tried to turn the focus back where it belonged — on him. He should have been talking about himself, but I had a lot of trouble getting him to do so.

As we talked, it became obvious that Ricardo was doing with me what he had always done with casting directors. Whenever they asked him about himself, Ricardo turned the question around and expressed interest in *them*. His first instinct was to take care of them. He would answer their questions by asking whether seeing actors all day long wasn't draining, or if the casting director got a lot of satisfaction out of what he or she did.

He would keep these conversations going for quite a long time, and would leave the interview thinking that he had done well. In one sense, he had. "I know the casting directors like me," Ricardo says, and he's right. They do like him. They just don't have any idea who he is or what he can do because they've been talking about themselves for the whole interview — and as a result, they don't give him parts.

When we started looking at the patterns in Ricardo's life, it became clear that he was a habitual caretaker. He had always played the role of father to his brothers and sisters, even though they were all older than he was, and he had also taken care of his mother. His father had almost never been around, so Ricardo had never received the fathering he craved. As we frequently do, he tried to give to other people the thing he wanted most for himself, hoping that it would be returned to him in time and that others would one day start looking after him. This was not a conscious "buying" of affection and caring; Ricardo had no idea why he did it. In fact, the first time he recognized this dynamic was in our session.

Being the caretaker also made Ricardo feel that he belonged. It had given him a clear function in his family, and it gave him a function in his career, or so he thought.

It has taken him thirty-five years to recognize that he is tired of relating to people in this way, and to admit that there are times when he wants to run away and become totally irresponsible and self-indulgent.

Much of our work together involved the child in Ricardo who wanted to be spoiled, pampered, and indulged. He needed to give his child the attention he craved, and to find safe ways of indulging that child — taking him to the movies, talking with him to find out what he wanted, even asking him what he wanted to wear each morning.

It was a revelation to Ricardo that he could give to himself what he had been hoping for from others all his life. As he got in touch with his need to be parented, the process of "adopting" and caring for his child became a major part of changing the way he handled himself, both professionally and personally.

Ricardo had a hard time learning not to apologize while giving his professional qualifications. Gradually, however, his passion for his work began to emerge in his presentation. As he got better at taking care of his child, and no longer tried to manipulate casting directors into taking care of him, they began to see him as an actor. He read for more roles and is now playing a number of far more challenging parts. He even plays mean and ugly characters, not just the "nice-guy" roles that used to come his way.

I have seen Ricardo's work since he started making these changes, and the results are dramatic. He maintains his own agenda and goes after what he wants. He no longer waits to see if he can help the other actors at his own expense, and other actors enjoy working with him more. They are no longer wary of him, as they were when they sensed his hidden agenda. His work is more spontaneous, with a relaxed, natural quality that it never had before.

Ricardo still has to be reminded occasionally to put himself first. Recently he had an opportunity to spend a day on the set of a television drama in New York. I asked him what he planned to say to the people there, and Ricardo replied, "Well, I'll thank them, of course, and tell them how much I enjoy their work."

"Isn't there anything you want from them?" I asked.

"A job," he laughed, as if this were quite a joke. Then he caught himself, frowned, and realized that he'd stumbled over the same old block. He said seriously, "I think I *will* ask about a job."

Commitment had always seemed selfish to Ricardo. Now he sees it as the cornerstone of his acting career. He is just as nice as he ever was — more so, in fact, because his caring is more genuine — but because he is more grounded in his own reality he commands more respect from himself and others.

Jessica: Acting her life

Jessica was a student in the Berkeley workshop mentioned at the beginning of this chapter. She wrote me this letter shortly after the workshop.

> The questions you asked individuals regarding their specific defense poses (i.e., "Why are you afraid of me?" "What are you angry about?" etc.) seemed to accomplish the most in discovering what *action* the actor could take to solve his or her problem. Your technique also enabled the individual to genuinely gauge the discrepancy between

what the projected self-image was, and what was actually received.

I know my focus of "selling myself" rather than "being myself" kept me from feeling vulnerable. When you pointed that out to me, I suddenly could feel myself in the present moment. It was a funny combination of shock ("Oh, no, now I've blown it, now she knows I don't know what I'm doing") and relief ("Good, now I can stop my 'strong actress' acting, which is hard work!").

It was interesting to note changes in body tensions. Every time an actor was trying to "perform" herself or himself, there was an incredible nervousness, hyper-responsiveness (without really listening to what you were saying), and a sense of desperation. But once you started the individual reflecting on his or her inward process, they relaxed into a very natural and intimate body language.

Your interview demanded an honest in-depth analysis of how we all project ourselves and also gave us a measure of accepting and integrating this new awareness into a more effective manner of communication.

At one point during the workshop you shared the comment that you still had the feelings inside that you felt as a small child. I realized that in exposing so much of yourself in such an accepting and sharing manner, you demonstrated what the whole interview process was about.

Some time after the workshop, Jessica came to me as a client. She wrote me the following letter after being cast in a major role in a film. She was looking back over the past several years.

Here are some thoughts on the process you've given me. Because my twin sister and I were moved around a lot when we were young (we went to thirteen different schools), we depended very much on one another to relay our shared sense of reality, which, more often than not, did not have too much in common with other people's. Our games of "Let's Pretend" were usually too intense for other children to be interested in them for very long, and because we had created such a complex and mutually per-ceived fantasy life, we ended up "performing" for each other in "real" life.

Consequently, I "observed" Daisy performing from an early age, and she "observed" my real life behavior. Our adolescence was a nightmare because we had to learn to divorce ourselves from the integral identity that we had shared . . . "the twins" . . . we learned to really hate that title. "Here come the twins." "Ask the twins." "Get the twins to do it." It was at this point that we both discovered acting.

Acting gave me the assurance that I was a separate, inter-esting, whole person, without relying on my twin's shared perceptions. I was always cast as "strong" characters — Antigone, Viola, Alma — and I really saw myself as needing to be "strong" and "whole" and "adult."

I also saw myself as a lot of other actresses do, without any other interests or assets, and anything or anyone out-side the theater was not part of my young vocabulary. I began a pattern of "performing" my personal life as though I were just offstage waiting to become a "real" actress. It was a sheltered existence, as any new informa-tion usually did not filter its way through my complex and "strong" ideas of who I was and where I was going.

When I first met you in Berkeley, I was very defensive about being a "good," "professional" actress. My ego was having a hard time going back to school, but I knew that my limitations were keeping me from enjoying my inner self, the one that I have kept carefully hidden. I was only bringing out those qualities that I can control and affect a calculated result with.

The thought that surprised me when I first met you was "I want her to like/approve of me so badly, I can't even see her," which was the first time I could remember not being able to perceive someone, because my own needs came first. I have no recollection of what I said, or what conclu-sion you may have had based on my behavior, but I remember you *really* looked at me. And that really affected me, that someone could really see me, and so I went home that night and tried to see me, and that started a very long process where I tried to teach myself how to become more sensitive; to perceive an environment, a person, a concept, a feeling, rather than to approach it with predetermined responses.

What our work together gave me was that I was able to become a participant, rather than a performer, in my own life.

Jessica's insights about how she used to "perform" for the world are accurate. When I first took her hand in the workshop and we introduced ourselves, I sensed a very strong, self-willed, and capable young woman. Although I was more than twice her age, I felt sure that she had a strength that I could never find.

What I saw physically was a tall, charming woman with soft brown hair and a gentle face. She looked as though she could be vulnerable and sensitive, but those qualities were far from what she projected. There seemed to be nothing in her that was undecided, nothing that was not strong. I felt that she needed nothing from me, and that even if I offered to help her, I would feel foolish because she so obviously did not need my help.

Working with Jessica revealed to me the thoroughness with which an actor can create himself or herself, even though that creation may be far from the truth. She was also courageous enough to let me know how much it mattered that I see through her pretense and that I like her.

Dwayne: Trying to stay in control

I first met Dwayne when I was casting a motion picture. He was in his midfifties at the time. I was looking for someone to play a midlevel corporate executive. Although it was not a major role, the character appeared in quite a lot of the film. This man needed to project an authoritative presence without many lines in the script to help him do so. In terms of symbols, he was "order and predictability," against which some very unpredictable and dangerous games were being played.

Dwayne is tall, slender, and blue-eyed. He came through the door, and in that first second I thought, "Looks like a possibility — we'll see." As he sat down, something in his look was challenging. It seemed to be saying, "I dare you to guess anything about who I am." It was not an air of intriguing mystery, but rather almost a sense of shiftiness, as if the ground I was walking on could move and change. I began to feel that what I was seeing was not really what was there. I wrote in my notes, "Uneasy."

I asked Dwayne to tell me something about himself. He told me about a number of New York stage plays he'd been in and about writer friends in whose work he had acted. His demeanor was self-assured but somehow unreal, and his smile was challenging. It seemed to say, "If you believe all this, then you are really being taken in," and at the same time, "If you *don't* believe all this, then you are really a bad person, a doubting person."

When I am casting a film, I go with my hunches. If I am feeling confused, I don't question that confusion — it's simply the way I feel. I figure that a lot of people would feel the same way if they were looking at a film of this person.

In this case, I felt that there was no time to fool around or play games, so I said, "I'm confused. I don't know what to believe about you. I feel that you are mocking me in some way. I'm not going to have you read. If you want to call me next week, I'll talk to you further about this. But now I have to see the next person."

Smiling strangely, he said, "You could be right. Maybe I *am* mocking you." And he left.

Rather than calling the next week, Dwayne sent me a letter that must have been very difficult to write, detailing his early life. His had been an unusual childhood. Everything he had thought about his immediate family had turned out to be untrue. The woman he had thought was his mother was actually his grandmother. The man he had thought was his father, whom he had thought was married to his "mother," had turned out to be a man his grandmother lived with for the first five years of

Dwayne's life. The person he had thought was his older sister was really his mother, whom he had never seen. She lived in New York, and was mentioned only in hushed tones. She was "on the stage," and that sounded glamorous. The rest of the family disapproved of her, yet she provided them with an endless and fascinating topic of conversation.

Dwayne had found out about these tangled relationships when he was around four, or at least about as much of it as a four-year-old could comprehend. When he was five, his real mother had returned home, swept him up, and established a new "home" for him, with three of her friends and a new extended family. This had been the most wonderful time in his life. All of his new family were in the theater, and he recalls them as vibrant, funny, and outgoing people who introduced him to an energized way of living that he had never before experienced. It didn't matter to him that some of his schoolmates' mothers wouldn't allow them to play with him because of his mother and her friends.

One day, near the end of that wonderful winter, his mother and her friends were not there when he came home from school. Instead, there was his grandmother, who told him that his mother had gone "on the road" with a show and that he was coming back to live with her. Dwayne's life went on like this, his home and family continually changing, for quite some time.

When Dwayne was nineteen, he joined the army in the hope that it would bring some order and discipline to his life. In some ways, it did. By the time I met him, however, he was out of the army and trying to figure out how to live and what to do with his life.

He had done some acting in the service. In fact, that was all the acting work he had ever done. But, since his life seemed to be full of lies anyway, he had felt that lying to me about Broadway and all the plays he had been in really wouldn't matter.

Here are some excerpts from the letter Dwayne sent me:

I always lie. Then I can always change the "truth" and thus never get caught investing my love or passion or any part of my work with anything that might be laughed at.

It is all lies anyway. When someone criticizes or applauds me, I still have the advantage of knowing that they have been taken in by something that may look like the truth at first glance, but it is actually a phantom fabric made up of lies.

You were right in what you said to me. I was challenging you to know that a lot of what I said was a lie. You did, and now I know that I have to do something about all this, but I am not sure what it is.

Dwayne's letter further revealed that just a few months earlier, a childhood friend had died. This friend had been the one constant in his life, and the only person to whom he did not lie. This had left Dwayne feeling much as he had felt the day his real mother had left him.

The erratic nature of his life had left Dwayne with a deep distrust of people and a need to control them. He felt that he could control casting directors to a degree by lying to them and by getting them off balance because then, no matter what they said to him, he could always reverse his position and regain control. He had tried to live his whole life this way, and it was not working on any level.

About six months after writing this letter, Dwayne called me to make an appointment for a consultation to begin the process of working through his painful past.

★   ★   ★

Most actors have work to do, either with a therapist or slowly, piece by piece, by themselves as Jessica did. If we carry around old emotional baggage, then that is what we will show to casting directors and agents — people who rarely have time to dig down below what they are shown, even if such digging might lead to gold.

One of the reasons we act is that we want to be seen and heard for who we really are, and part of our job is to present just that to the casting director. He or she needs to see us from the center of ourselves, not from some made-up version of what we think is wanted. When we "act" our lives in interviews, we put both ourselves and the casting director at a disadvantage.

When I am casting a film, I am perfectly happy when an actor says, "I feel really nervous right now." That's fine with me. Of course they are nervous. It's smarter for them to acknowledge it than to try to hide it.

Casting directors, agents, and directors love good acting and skilled craftspeople. They love the work, but they really don't know an actor well until they have spent a lot of time with him or her. All the energy that actors spend trying to "make him or her like me" is usually wasted.

By the same token, when we are not cast, we may think, "They rejected me." No, they didn't. They rejected our work for this particular role. We may simply have been too tall, or too like the lead, or too good-looking, or too something.

The casting director's skill has been built up over the years, just as the actor's has. She is able to extract an enormous amount of intuitive information from just a few words, in a few seconds. She gets a "hit" on someone, and that is what she works with. She has an enhanced awareness of these impressions, and their accuracy is what makes the top casting directors much sought after. Directors and producers say of these people, "They don't waste our time; they have great instincts." In many ways, they do the same kind of work that actors do: They rely on instinct and intuition.

chapter 8
The Secret of Absorbing a Script

It has always fascinated me that some actors can read a scene once and immediately grasp both its form and its substance, while others must struggle to learn their lines and to capture the emotional essence of the same scene.

Over the years I have thought about and experimented with this phenomenon, and I have come up with a method of internalizing and assimilating a ten-page script in one reading. I call it *absorbing a script.*

I stumbled onto this method almost by accident. For the workshops I present, we need scenes that are fairly short yet go somewhere dramatically, so I read many scripts to find scenes that will work. Because I have to read so many scripts so quickly, I can only read each one once. After I've selected the scenes, I usually don't look at them again until the workshop begins, when copies are passed out to participants before they do the scenes on videotape.

To my surprise, I began to find that, without referring to the script, I could prompt the actors whenever they lost their lines, even though I had looked at the scene only once. That is, I could prompt the scene *if I didn't think about it.* If I consciously tried to remember what the lines were, I lost them completely. My intellect, or left brain, simply would not or could not retrieve them. From the eyebrows up, which was where I was accustomed to finding information that I had "learned" or "memorized," I would draw a total blank. But some other part of me could recall the lines without effort.

Actors in the workshop commented on the fact that I seemed to know all these scripts. When I told them that I hadn't learned them, they replied that yes, I must have, because I could prompt them in any scene.

I continued to pay attention to what was happening. I didn't "know" the lines so much as "feel" them. If I didn't think, they would just come out of my mouth. As I spoke those lines, I always felt the emotions attached to them in the scene. These two elements—the memory and the feeling—seemed to be linked.

Since my only contact with the script had been during that first reading, it must have been then that the absorption had happened. I don't have a photographic memory, so that wasn't the answer. I began to think about how I had read the scripts and how this was different from the way I would read if someone handed me a scene and said, "Learn this."

I discovered that I had read these scenes as if I were living the script—seeing, smelling, and feeling everything, being present in the moment and experiencing deeply everything that took place. My left brain, the logical, reasoning part of me, was doing very little—hardly thinking at all. By the time I had finished reading, I knew without thinking and in great detail everything that had happened—in the same way I "know" things that I have experienced in my own life.

If I later did the scene with another actor, I felt all of the implications of the other role and its effect on my character; however, I seldom had any knowledge of my own lines until I "felt" the moment through hearing my scene partner's lines. This had an additional advantage; it forced me to stay in the moment and listen, rather than go hunting around for my line while he was saying his. I could not get my lines unless I heard his in my gut.

This was not at all how I had thought "memorization" worked. Memorizing had always meant pacing around repeating the lines over and over, or writing them down by hand to get them "in." This new way of memorizing was so easy and even enjoyable that I decided to try an experiment to find out if it worked with other actors.

Now, before I start a seminar on this method of absorbing a script, I always warn the participants that I will ask them to abandon everything they have ever learned about learning. I tell them that nothing is going to feel the same. The way in which they have previously learned lines will be of no use to them. They will have to focus entirely on how they feel, trusting that the feelings will give them the lines.

The information presented here has been acquired over the years. The people in the Denver Experiment were the first to help me learn it.

The Denver Experiment

I had been working with a group of actors in Denver for some time, and I asked ten of them to give me a Sunday. I chose actors with whom I felt comfortable enough to risk complete failure. I also knew that these people would give this new idea a try, just to find out what it was all about.

I opened the workshop by saying, "I think I have found a way to learn a script in one reading."

There was silence for a moment, then, "Okay, show us."

I handed out the first script, which was three pages long, without assigning roles. I gave these instructions:

"Read the script through slowly on as deep a level as possible, seeing and feeling everything that takes place. If it is in a restaurant, *be* in that restaurant. See and feel and hear and smell what it is like. Create your own version of the restaurant. It doesn't matter if it is the same one your scene partner will be in. Every word on the page means something, so don't skip over anything. If you are aware that you're thinking, 'That's a long speech,' or if you find yourself wondering what happens next, then you have stopped feeling and started thinking. Stop reading, breathe deeply, and go back to feeling the script again."

When the actors had finished reading that first script, I took back the pages. It was difficult for some hands to let go of the papers. People had a dazed look, and someone said, "I have no idea what I just read."

I asked, "In the script, where are we?"

"In Grace's kitchen," everyone answered immediately. That was easy enough.

"What's the first line?"

Everyone said it in unison, and the next line, and the one after that. They knew just what Grace was doing and when the action took place. Some of the actors seemed more at home with this process than others, but by the end of the scene everyone was joining in and even correcting small details. There was tremendous certainty and enthusiasm, and I began to get excited about our success.

We planned to videotape the next scene. Again, everyone read the new script slowly and deeply, and then I took the pages back. They all sat frozen, looking as if they were afraid that, if they moved or talked, they would lose everything they had just absorbed. When I spoke, I could tell they all just wanted me to be quiet. Their looks said, "If I listen to anything you say, I'll forget everything I just read, so don't say anything." One person actually said, "I'm not sure that I know anything I just read, but I do know I can't speak to you."

The actors sat looking as if they were carrying something that would spill if they so much as moved or thought of anything else. They had no idea where all this material was being stored, but one thing was sure: It was not in their left brains, where lines they had just learned were usually kept.

If they searched where they were used to searching for such material, they found nothing. They realized that they had to wait until they were actually involved in the scene, until the feelings of the scene were activated, before any lines were available to them. When they finished the scene, some looked dazed and said things like, "Did we do it all?" or "That felt great. I don't know where I was, but it felt great."

Those first scenes we taped were slow, but they had a strong sense of feeling and emotion—much more than we would usually see in the first runthrough of conventionally learned material. We were all amazed and pleased when we saw the tapes. Several people said that this was the best tape they had ever done.

To me, the tapes were interesting because of what was *not* there. The anxiety, the eyes that darted around "looking" for lines, the stiff muscles in the face that obscure real emotion, the tension that makes the viewer uneasy—all were absent. Also gone was the tendency to look like frightened animals whenever they felt uncertain. The feelings we saw on tape were always appropriate and never forced.

I was also intrigued that many of the elements that normally take weeks to put in place—the shadings, timing, and emotional nuances—were there from the very beginning on a feeling level. The performances also seemed to be immune to such internal chatter as "I have to get this right," "I can't remember where I put the coffee mug down," and all the other problems that crop up in first runthroughs.

We decided to try it again, and the second script we taped turned out to be the worst of the day. Most people agreed that they had done one of two things:

1. They had said to themselves, "This is easy," and had not brought the same level of concentration to this reading as they had to the first one. They had slipped into thinking, "Oh, this is a snap; I'll just zip through it." The results were dreadful. The depth of feeling that was the secret of success in the first reading had disappeared in the second reading.
2. They had consciously or unconsciously gone halfway back to the way they had always learned scripts, mixing left-brain memorization with right-brain absorption, because they thought the success of the first experiment might have been a fluke and they wanted to get it "right." They found that the two methods didn't mix well, and in fact produced some of the most uncertain work they had ever done.

With the second script out of the way, we went on. The work became more and more fluid, and the speed of the scenes picked up. I was delighted when someone said, "I always felt that acting should be like this. It feels like there is nothing between me and what I see on the tape — no defenses, nothing. It's easy, it's really easy. Did I say that?"

By the end of the day, five scripts later, we were all exhausted, but we knew that we were onto something. Now we had a tool that we could use in readings for casting directors or on film sets when given new pages to learn for the same day.

And this method wasn't just fast; it also produced better results than the conscious memorization process. All the actors felt that they knew more about their characters, more quickly, than they ever had through the intellectual, layer-by-layer discovery process that they usually went through. They seemed to have an instinct for who their characters were and could bypass much of the "study" part of understanding those characters. All the information they needed was simply there on an intuitive level.

Later in the day, we discovered that it was possible to go into scenes learned by this method to make adjustments, to work on detail and timing, and to include the new work when the scene was done again — *if* the scene were read again with the new method after the adjustments were made. If it were not read again in this way, then part of the scene would still be in the experiential or right part of the actor's brain, while the adjustments would be in the left brain. This resulted in confusion and uncertainty. But if the whole piece were read again deeply, there was no confusion, and all the improvements were in place.

Absorbing a script from inside one's own experience obviously works, but how long does the memory last? So far, we know that it lasts at least three years. I can still throw the first line of a scene to any of the actors who did the first Denver workshop, and they can pick it up and go with it.

That first day in Denver, we did scripts of up to five pages. It didn't seem to make any difference how long or how short the scene was; the results were the same. In subsequent workshops, we have been successful with ten- and twelve-page scenes.

Right-Brain Learning

This method of absorbing a script with the right brain may feel strange at first, but only because we are used to using our left brains for the task of memorizing scripts.

Actually, we use our right brains to learn many things. The first time we drive to a friend's house, we may be glued to a piece of paper telling us to take a right at the gas station and a left after the shopping center, but a week or a month later the pattern is part of us. We might not be able to name any of the streets along the way, or even to describe the route accurately to someone else, but we "feel" when to turn.

The first time we cook a complicated recipe, we may be slaves to the cookbook, referring back to it at every step. The next time we prepare that dish, we can go along for quite a while without having to check the recipe.

Although the theory of right and left brain was explored earlier in the book, it is crucial to what follows, so I would like to repeat a little of it here.

When creative work is going on, the right and left hemispheres of the brain are synchronized and working with each other. The right brain is sending the left enormous amounts of emotionally charged material, and the left is rapidly sorting and routing messages. When this synchronized communication is functioning well, we don't have to think consciously to arch one eyebrow or place a hand on a hip and then say, "Well?" This is all taken care of in the message from the right brain, which comes complete with movement, expression, and all the emotion required. It therefore stands to reason that if we can absorb scripts into the right brain, then the left brain will do what it does best — route into the performance all the richness of material delivered to it.

Unfortunately, in most systems of education, the left brain becomes charged with the responsibility for the conscious learning process. Its ability to repeat the material learned has been reinforced by the system of grading, and this method has proved to be effective, but there is a great deal of creative work and learning that does not respond to this technique.

What the right brain has absorbed often remains unconscious or unknown until it actually appears or is used. We have to trust it. It is difficult to "examine" and therefore difficult to grade. That is why it is impossible to use grades in comparing one actor to another. We can say of ourselves, "That feels like some of the better work I have done." Others can say whether or not *they* are moved by it. But that is all.

Knowing where the mark on a stage is and hitting it, knowing when we're supposed to pick up the coffee mug—these are logical left-brain activities. They are essential, but they are not what make great actors.

As a young actress, I was always told, "Learn your lines, you'll be fine." I began to think that if I learned my lines well enough, I would be a good actress. I often felt that I only existed from the eyebrows up. Just learning my lines did nothing to cultivate my emotional approach to the play or to integrate all the words and feelings so that I felt them in my body.

Absorbing a script seems to lodge it in our hearts and bodies as well as in our minds. It allows us to use the vast resources of the right brain, which can store, catalogue, and process huge masses of information with their associated feelings, and then retrieve them at will.

Over the years I have experimented with absorbing longer and longer pieces of material. I've found that this is the best way to come to terms with what a stage script is about and what it "feels" like, and it has proved a great way to do the first read. The same is true for film scripts. After reading a script for the first time at a deep, intensive experiential level I have found that I have a knowingness about it upon which I can safely base my ensuing work, whether it is as an actress or director. I then break the script down into smaller pieces and absorb them again through this method and begin to work in detail, although I find that my knowingness supplies almost all the detail I need.

The keys to success with this method are trust, patience, and persistence in staying with the feelings even when it is uncomfortable to do so. This method involves trusting a whole new part of ourselves. It means staying absolutely in the moment and being open to our feelings.

Many actors find themselves in tears after first doing a scene this way. Mary, who took a Denver workshop, said, "I always knew it should feel like that." Watching a videotape of himself, Jack said, "I look like I have always felt inside. I've never seen myself look that good before."

In talking with artists in other disciplines, it appears that this is exactly what happens when a dancer is following a dance captain, when a pianist is at peak form, when a sculptor is uncovering what is inside the material, and when a ceramicist is feeling the way to a new form. Technique, form, and concept all work together.

It seems to me that this right-brain method of absorbing a script is an economical, truthful, consistent, and enlivening way for actors to work. Clients have told me that it makes them more relaxed in interviews, readings, auditions, and performances. They actually enjoy these parts of their work now.

The reward for being as vulnerable as we must be to absorb a script is an openness and awareness that take our performances to a whole new level.

The Value of Discomfort

This technique of absorbing a script often brings up uncomfortable feelings, both because this way of learning is so new and because it taps into powerful gut-level feelings. In fact, this unavoidable discomfort can be valuable to our work.

During the first half hour of every workshop I lead, while we are getting the first take of the actors' scenes on tape, I always feel ineffective and "disjointed." These feelings show that the commitment to the work, no matter how long we have been practicing it, must be made afresh each time. At each workshop, I struggle through some of the old doubts about my own ability. If I recognize these doubts and this struggle, then they are accepted and welcomed as a necessary part of the process. It is almost as if they are the gateway to my own freedom, and I must pass through them to get to what I want.

As actors, we must pass through this discomfort whenever we tackle an emotional block, learn a new skill, or begin work on a scene. This initial discomfort can also be a powerful acting tool, giving scenes a reality they might otherwise lack. Just as my uncle advised staying in one place if I became lost, we should stay with our discomfort until it dissolves, not trying to push it away or hide from it. So many scenes are meant to be filled with discomfort; we try to smooth them out, to make them seamless, when they should be just as "bumpy" as we feel.

If I could say only one thing to actors about their work, it would be TRUST YOUR GUT. We may not "know" with the left brain where an instinct comes from or how to justify it, but we can trust that the intuition and emotion of the right brain are the fuel of good performances. These are the rewards we gather when we have reconnected with our creative center; the process of absorbing a script can help us put those rewards to use in our work.

chapter 9
How to Eat an Elephant

How do you eat an elephant? The answer, of course, is one mouthful at a time, *concentrating on that mouthful* and not on the elephant.

This chapter helps to dispel the overwhelming vision of the elephant — what I call the "specter of success" — and looks at ways to concentrate on each mouthful, from setting small, attainable goals to ensuring that our environment supports our work.

The Specter of Success

Success has two qualities that are extremely difficult to manage: It is *big*, and it is *vague*.

Because it is vague, we often think of ourselves as failures simply because we have no evidence that we are successful. Yet when pressed for details about exactly what "success" means, we don't really know. Perhaps we are lucky, and good at our craft, and we earn an enormous amount on a successful film. Still, inside we may feel, "Yes, but what I really secretly long to do is to star in a Broadway play." As long as "that" is ahead, success is still ahead as well, no matter what we may have achieved or how the world evaluates us.

Most of us start out dreaming big. Seldom does anyone begin an acting career saying, "Oh, maybe I'll get a day or two on a soap opera, or a couple of commercials." We are much more likely to dream of our future in terms of playing Othello or Lady Macbeth or the lead in an Academy-Award-winning film. There's nothing wrong with these dreams; in fact, they are essential. It's just that there is such a great distance between where we are now and where we dream of being that it's hard to know what all the steps in between look like. In fact, that's one reason that some of those near and dear to us become anxious about our career. We can't tell them what we are going to do next.

For actors, "the dream" or "success" can take many forms and can happen in any number of strange ways. We aren't climbing steadily up some corporate ladder with the next twenty or thirty years all planned out for us, including clear job titles, raises in pay, vacations, and steadily increasing levels of status and responsibility.

Instead, we proceed in fits and starts, sometimes crawling along and at other times making quantum leaps. Our progress is unpredictable, and so is the direction in which it takes us. "Big breaks" do happen, but more often the achievements are bite size. Our career sometimes seems to move like a tortoise and sometimes like a hare.

Where to Start

Three elements are necessary to creativity:

1. The recognition of the challenge.
2. The commitment to the challenge.
3. The perception that we have some degree of control over what we are going to do.

Without all three of these elements, nothing happens.

We have seen the elephant. It is indeed a challenge; it is also seductive—we want it, and we are a little afraid of it. The next step is our commitment to eat the elephant: "I am an actor; I am going to make a career of this." How? "Well, I guess, take the first mouthful." We have started. Reading this book, taking a class, looking in the classified ads, going to your first community theater audition, playing your first major role in a feature film, my requesting information about the Old Vic Theatre School or sending this book to the first publisher (it was rejected) — these are all mouthfuls. With each mouthful, we perceive that we can actually do this; we can live this life that we so desire.

In order to eat the elephant of our career, we have to break it down into smaller, more manageable pieces. This gives us a place to start, a beginning to the journey. Everyone's journey is different. Two actors with Broadway dreams may both end up on Broadway, but their paths toward that goal will not be the same. We have to trust our own path.

There are parts of an acting career — the more practical and political parts — for which we can set goals. We can say to ourselves that we will learn to tap dance, or get a new résumé printed, or learn to juggle, or get new pictures, or send out a hundred new tapes. Each of these goals has an end point that can be attained. Each is a mouthful of the elephant, and each helps to build our commitment to and confidence in our chosen career.

Bonnie: Reclaiming the dream

Bonnie lives in Colorado, and her dream has always been to act — to appear in leading roles, maybe on Broadway someday. She has worked in summer stock and made several commercials, but to support herself she has also acquired office skills. Over the years the office jobs, her co-workers, and the things that a steady salary has allowed her to buy have come to seem almost more important than her work as an actress. As her emphasis on acting has lessened, Bonnie has become more and more depressed; she is increasingly hard on herself for not doing what she wants to do.

When she first came to see me, Bonnie hated her office job because it was not acting, hated herself for not being more involved in acting, and almost hated acting because it was what had driven her to acquire the skills for the office job in the first place. She had enough money and time to take acting courses, but she wasn't doing so.

Her first steps were to take an improvisation class and learn to tap dance, something she had always wanted to do. Within a couple of weeks, things looked a lot better. We worked on looking at her job as something that enabled her to act, not something that prevented her from acting. Bonnie has moved back toward her path again. She is doing something about her dream. She has started a savings account that is labeled "passport to acting" in her mind. At some point in the not-too-distant future, she will take a leave of absence and return to the summer theater where she used to work—a manageable dream, one mouthful of the elephant.

★   ★   ★

We have to concentrate on bite-size pieces, not on the whole elephant, and work toward the specific, smaller items on our list. We can't worry about achieving success or about being perfect. We can only do the task that is before us: one class, one phone call, one interview, learning one role or one new skill.

We have to trust that each step is part of our path. Later, when we look back, we may say, "Of *course* I had to do it that way. I didn't realize it at the time, but if it hadn't happened just that way, I wouldn't be where I am today."

The key is to *do something*. No effort is ever wasted. As long as we sit contemplating the elephant, nothing will happen except that the elephant will seem bigger and tougher. Taking one step, accomplishing one item on our list, gives us a forward motion, an involvement in the process, that makes it easier to take the next step.

Asking for Help and Information

Asking questions is almost never a mistake. We can think of each question asked as a mouthful of the elephant eaten. We may be afraid that people will think we're stupid, but they are more likely to be both flattered and impressed. It's perfectly acceptable to ask people we admire how they got started, and what advice and recommendations they have for us.

It is easy to feel that we should already know things. Often it seems as though everyone knows all the answers except us. Most experienced actors are happy to answer questions about how they got started, and many in the industry feel that they have a duty to the profession to hand on the information they've acquired from experience or been given by someone else. It doesn't matter if we sometimes choose the wrong person or the wrong time and get brushed off. It's all right to ask again and again. Everyone was a beginner at some point.

Once we start asking questions, we often find that they have simple answers. We've been missing the answers not because the questions are so difficult but because we haven't been asking them. Either we didn't know who to ask, or we were afraid to ask the people we thought would know, or we were afraid of appearing stupid and feeling that we didn't belong.

When I was working as West Coast casting director for the film *Smooth Talk,* I could tell clearly from the interviews and readings which actors would do well in motion pictures or stage work and which ones probably wouldn't. It didn't have so much to do with talent, because nearly all of these actors were talented; it had to do with personal security and the knowledge that asking questions could produce valuable information and didn't imply blame or stupidity. Those who would succeed were those who wanted to know what was going on and who were confident enough to ask.

All of these actors were about fifteen years old. They came into the office, read for me, and had a Polaroid taken. Some of them left immediately and, I felt sure, thought that now the whole matter was out of their control. Others stayed around and asked, "What happens next?" "Will you need me again?" "I'm going to be away next week, is it all right if I call?" "Would you like another photograph?"

These were kids who knew how to ask for what they wanted, and that reinforced my confidence in them. They earned my respect. They were open to accepting help and to being supported by others in their professional lives. Such respect, affection, and caring make for powerful bonds in the complex worlds of theater and motion pictures.

Asking questions is important even after we've landed the role. If what we're doing isn't working, we need to find out from the director what *will* work. George Bernard Shaw was once asked for advice by a man who was directing one of his own plays at the Abbey Theatre in Dublin. Shaw answered in a long, detailed letter that was published in a small book entitled *The Art of Rehearsal*. Shaw wrote, "Any fool can tell you something is wrong. Don't tell an actor that something is wrong unless you can tell him why it is wrong and what to do to make it right. It takes a person of perception, understanding, and sometimes near genius to tell him why it is wrong. If you don't know, shut up."

We can't count on all directors to follow Shaw's advice, but we can be responsible for trying to find out not just what is wrong but also what we can do to correct it.

In this process, we mustn't forget to ask ourselves what feels right to us. Sometimes the answer is only a faint shred of feeling, a soft whisper, but it will grow stronger if we listen and if we trust what comes from within us.

Staying Flexible

Sometimes it seems as if fate sees that things are going well for us and then mockingly hands us something to upset all our plans. Maybe someone in our family gets ill and we have to leave a booming career to go back home for a while. We must learn how to be flexible and how to continue our work in some way or other. If we don't, our lives will become even more chaotic.

Greta: Finding new ways to be her creative self

Greta lives on a farm in the Midwest. She was an actress before her marriage and well on her way, working almost all the time. She now has three small children. In the earlier years of her marriage, she was able to work in community theater and sum- mer stock. In the last year, however, she has moved much farther away from town, and, with three small children, these outlets are no longer available to her.

When I first saw her, she was very depressed and hated almost everything about her life. She agreed to start writing for an hour every day, beginning with monologues that she could present as audition pieces, and now she is working on a one-act play.

Although writing is not her first love, the fact that she is doing *something* every day has restored her belief in herself as a creative artist, and this makes her feel much more at ease with this period in her life. In eighteen months the family will be moving to town, and she will be able to act again. Greta is eating a piece of the elephant, perhaps not the piece she dreamed she would be eating right now, but she is continuing her work.

PAY ATTENTION TO ★ ★ ★ CHANGES

Sometimes we are tempted to think that we should have started on a different piece of the elephant. We compare our progress with that of another actor; we feel that we are doing it wrong, or that we're not getting anywhere. The truth is that we never progress in neat uniform steps, nor are any two actors' lives alike. Whatever piece of the elephant we choose is the "right" piece for us to be working on now.

On the other hand, nothing on our list of small, manageable goals is written in stone. Nor do the tasks on the list need to be accomplished in the order in which we first wrote them down. Our instincts for change deserve as much trust as the original items on the list. By staying flexible, we allow our list of attainable goals to serve and support us, rather than letting it become a whip with which to beat ourselves up. If some task or goal feels wrong, we can switch to something that feels right. There are many crossroads along each actor's path; at each of them, we can choose which route we want to take.

The Other Parts of the Actor's Life

We don't do good work when we are anxious about money, relationships, health, living situations, or family. Life is full of stress, and we will never live completely free from anxiety, but we can eliminate obviously destructive people, behaviors, and situations from our lives. The following sections look at the need to ensure that the other parts of our lives support and honor our work as actors. Creating a supportive environment is one way to give our work the priority it deserves. When we are focused on what is most important to us, life automatically becomes less confusing.

Working at "other jobs"

At some point, most of us have "other jobs" that pay the rent while we develop and become established in our own creative career. The point of having these jobs is to support our creativity, to give us the money we need to continue living while we do our "real" work, take classes, practice, read, and hone our craft.

Sometimes, however, we forget that these "other jobs" are secondary to our creative work and are taken in the service of our creative work. We lose sight of the fact that we have them in order to do what we really want to do, and one of two things happens. We may begin to think that the "other job" defines who we really are — we say, "Well, I act a little on the side," rather than, "I'm an actor, and from time to time I support myself by doing other things." Or the "other job" becomes a tremendous burden. "I have to go to *work* now," we moan. If the job is such a burden, then acting becomes a burden too, because we wouldn't have to have that job if it weren't for acting.

We can't win in this situation. The job's not working well, and the creative work isn't getting done. We get down on ourselves because we start to think that if we were better at acting, we wouldn't have to have the job in the first place. This kind of thinking can send us into a downward spiral.

We need to remind ourselves that the job is something that enables us to do what we want to do; therefore it has its own value. Like Bonnie, earlier in this chapter, we must learn to say to the child within, "That's fifty dollars more toward the summer session we are going to take." Changing our perspective will take a little work, but we can teach ourselves to focus on the positive and to see the "other job" in the context of our *real* work.

"I *have* a real job: I'm an actor"

On the other hand, there are people who don't have an "other job" to pay the bills and who may be struggling to make a living as actors. Well-meaning family and friends often say, "Why don't you get a real job?" or "Don't daydream so much; sometimes I think you're in another world." We *are* in another world. That's who we are and, unless we're willing to give up our work, that's who we will remain. We, and they, might as well get used to it and give our work the respect it demands.

Say it — over and over: "I *have* a real job: I'm an actor."

Establishing a supportive living situation

Other professionals have offices or designated places to work. We have to do our daily work somewhere, but much of it is not done on the stage or on the film set; it is done at home. That means our home must be both a retreat and a place to work. We may need to have a place where we can work with a video camera or rehearse without creating havoc in other people's lives. If this isn't the case now, we need to find a creative solution, or else to consider the possibility of moving, no matter how much we would like to live with these people. It's a question of priorities.

Different kinds of housemates call for different kinds of solutions. I've known several actors who lived in group situations where they couldn't work on scenes or monologues with a camera or tape recorder because they disturbed other people; or else there was so much noise in the house that they themselves were distracted. They would get very upset: "I just can't work in that place. There's too much chaos, and people get on my back if I rehearse."

When I asked Ronnie why she continued living in a situation like this, she looked at me as if I were insane. "But Matt [her boyfriend] lives there!" Again, it's a question of priorities and creative solutions. Maybe Matt would consider moving to a place with enough room to support Ronnie's pursuit of her work. If he won't, maybe she needs to reexamine the relationship. It's also possible that Ronnie is using the living situation as an excuse to avoid doing her work.

My client Tom said that there was no privacy where he lived with four other people, and that the only place where he could rehearse scenes was in the bathroom. "I have to go into the john and lock the door to work on a monologue," he said, "and all the time I'm wondering if they can hear me, and I'm thinking I hate being in the john to do my work. I'm beginning to hate my work."

Working in the bathroom has given Tom a dozen reasons why his work isn't very good. He feels cramped and constricted. He doesn't feel good about the fact that he can only do his work in a bathroom, that he only has one little corner of the house in which to pursue his dreams, and that even there he has to worry about being a nuisance to people.

Tom needs to change this situation, whether his solution is to move to a new place or to find a place outside his home in which to do his work—perhaps a studio that he can rent with other actors.

These kinds of changes aren't always comfortable, emotionally or financially, but we need to make them if creativity is really our top priority.

Asking for support from our families

There may be times—having three small children at home, for instance—when it is difficult to find enough time to do our creative work. But even under these circumstances, we have to do *something*. This may mean hiring a baby-sitter five hours a week and taking tap dancing lessons or learning to play the piano. The person who will help us take that time for ourselves is the child within. He or she needs that time, and we need to promise our child that we will spend a certain amount of time each day on creative activities. Then let him or her help us keep to that discipline: "You slept in again today. You promised we were going to rehearse this morning. What about tomorrow?"

Dealing with our own parents can also be difficult. Parents often have misgivings when we choose artistic careers because we don't usually bring in a steady salary. Our lives often lack the financial security that they naturally want for their children.

We have to be realistic about our parents' attitudes and involvement in our career. If they seem extremely unhappy, uncomfortable, or unsure about our career in acting, perhaps we should not insist that they attend every performance.

We have to let go of needing their approval. We can let them know about performances, but we have to allow them to make up their own minds about coming to see our work. They may be interested in our career, and they may not. At some point in the future, they may suddenly become fascinated with what we do, but until then we have to go our own way and let them go theirs. Their approval would be nice, but it is not essential to our happiness or success.

Again, we need to keep an eye on the child inside us. If we feel on a fundamental level that we're doing something of which our parents don't approve, the rebellious teenager may start acting out. Or the scared child may want parental approval badly enough to abandon the creative work. Since there is a part of us that will always want to act, this could set up a tremendous internal battle.

The more independent and secure we become about our work, the more likely it is that our family will support us — but that support always needs to come from ourselves first.

Dealing with friends' responses

Sometimes friends outside the arts don't understand why we do what we do. I recently left my home near San Francisco to spend two months directing a play in New York. When my friends heard about this project, some asked, "Why do you have to go to New York to direct a play? Don't you mind being gone?" Of course a part of me minded being gone, but a much bigger part of me wanted to go.

In "normal" professions, time tends to be divided between the workplace and the home. People work at the office and play or relax at home. In the creative arts, these environments are less distinct; it's difficult to turn creativity on and off just by changing locale.

Some artists find that they work better if they make an extra effort *not* to bring work home, if they have a place where absolutely no work is done and where their only job is to relax. Others like the merging of work and play. The important thing is to determine what balance works for each of us and to set up both work and home environments so that they support us. It's also important to explain to those concerned — both at home and at work — the distinctions we have chosen to make.

Sometimes friends become jealous of our success. We expect our friends to support us, and the disappointment and loss of trust we experience when they don't can be very painful.

It's likely that the jealousy has less to do with us than with some unresolved part of our friends' own processes. We can talk about it with them, and perhaps, after expressing some of their feelings, they can let go of their jealousy. Perhaps we can all learn to live with it and go on being friends. On the other hand, the jealousy may get in the way so much that we have to put the friendship on hold until we can all deal with it better.

When we find ourselves in such a situation, the important thing is to tell the truth, to say what we are feeling, and to keep the lines of communication open. It's also important to do what supports ourselves and our work. We don't have to run over people's feelings with a truck, but neither can we allow them to get in the way of our work.

It doesn't always happen, and it doesn't *have* to happen, but sometimes we lose friends when we succeed. Loneliness is a feeling that frequently accompanies success. All we can do is to feel it and try to understand it. For instance, the loneliness may be due to the fact that we feel distanced from our old friends while we are so deeply involved in our creative work. It can also be related to the letdown that accompanies the achievement of a long-held goal. (Both of these feelings are discussed later in this chapter.) If we can start the next project or pursue some aspect of the work that has always fascinated us, some of the loneliness will be dispelled.

Looking for supportive relationships

Our romantic relationships are often the last area of our lives that we are willing to change in order to create a more supportive environment for ourselves. The support of a lover or spouse can provide an incredible amount of momentum; sabotage by the same person — intended or unintended, conscious or unconscious — can be equally damaging.

Significant others often feel threatened by our relationship with acting. They treat it as they would a rival lover, and they treat us as they would if we were having an affair with someone else. All the anger, cajoling, seduction, and manipulation that we might expect in a love triangle can occur in the triangle made up of our mates, our acting, and us.

It is not uncommon for people to spend years clinging to unsupportive relationships or to relationships that have been over for some time, all the while complaining that they can't work because they are in a horrible relationship. Sometimes they are afraid of being alone, and sometimes they are simply afraid to confront their creative work.

The only solution in such a situation is to make a decision. If compromises have been tried and it seems that there is no way to have both the relationship and our acting work, then we must choose between the two.

Getting help from support groups

There are two kinds of support groups: those that offer emotional or psychological support and are open to all people, and those that are formed specifically for creative people as a place to talk about their work.

The first kind includes Alcoholics Anonymous, Adult Children of Alcoholics, Debtors Anonymous, AIDS support groups, men's or women's groups, and so on. Participation in these groups is strictly a matter of individual choice. If they appeal to us and we find them valuable, we can belong to them for as long as we feel they are helpful.

The other kind of support group is usually put together by artists for artists. One option for groups of creative people whose members are in the same or associated disciplines is to hire a therapist or facilitator to help deal with work-related issues, blocks to progress, and recurring problems. The group creates its own ground rules, including how much to pay the leader, what subjects will be discussed, and so on. Nothing is written in stone here; the format can be changed at any time.

It's a good idea for the leader of the group to be familiar with the disciplines involved, and he or she should definitely understand the creative process. In addition, it must be made clear that the group members want to work through blocks, not to be "fixed" or made more "normal."

Such support groups can be the key to ensuring that all aspects of our lives honor and facilitate our work.

Understanding Sex and the Creative Process

Working with another actor on a new project produces an energy that is very similar to sexual energy, and feelings that are similar to falling in love. In fact, in a sense we do "fall in love" with our new family, the people with whom we are struggling to bring a new work into being. We are consumed by what we are doing artistically, and the lengthy process of getting to know one another is bypassed by our shared commitment. Our mutual work is more real than anything else. We are bonding in an intense situation — at least for the time being.

Most of us are literally physically turned on when we are working, and we need and want to feel this way. Most of the time we are able to channel that juicy, tingling, alive sexual energy into our work. Sometimes, though, it is directed at someone we are working with. If neither person is attached in real life, this can be a wonderful time. But these feelings can arise even if we are very much attached to a mate.

How does this happen? Both of us are pouring our hearts and souls into the project, discovering together each day how to make it work better. In a sense, no one knows us as well as that other person — at least for that brief time and in that particular creative way. Our mate isn't there when we are finding those brilliant solutions, but our creative partner is. And creative work demands passion and vulnerability, so we're likely to be feeling passionate and vulnerable as we work.

The intensity of the creative process can isolate actors from our usual lives. Many find it hard to be sexually attracted to anyone outside the process during that time. We may spend a sixteen-hour day on the film set, go home, eat, and go to bed so that we can get up and go back to the set early the next morning. During such periods, the time spent on the set is much more "real" than our home life. If we come home and our spouse says, "The plumber was here today," we think, "Huh?" The fact that we made a particular scene work with our partner is much more important, and much more seductive.

Unless we are free to engage in an actual romance, it's probably best not to act on these feelings but to wait until after the project is over and see what happens then. More often than not, the intense feelings will dissipate, and we will be left with a good friend with whom we have shared a rich and meaningful creative experience. If the romantic feelings *don't* go away, then we can deal with them in the context of the rest of our lives, rather than in the heat of the creative moment. Certainly these feelings can be *enjoyed,* whether or not we decide to act on them.

Falling in love with a fellow actor can be the best thing that can happen to a show, as it gives us all that magic and chemistry to bring to the work. But, in deciding what to do about these feelings, we should remember that we will serve the show best if we can stay sane and focused, rather than becoming distracted and guilty.

After the show or the project is over, we usually pick up our outside lives again, and the people who were dear to us before become dear again. Our focus shifts back to where it was before the project began, and the weeks or months we spent working on it can be seen in perspective for the wonderful transitory times they were.

Negotiating Contracts and Getting Paid

Money is a very tangible form of support, and for many of us it's the biggest, toughest part of the elephant. Trouble may arise when there doesn't seem to be enough money, or even when there seems to be almost too much.

Money issues often surface in the process of negotiating contracts. Here we have to stay focused on taking care of ourselves and honoring our work. Most creative artists hate dealing with contracts. They don't even want to know what's in them; they just want them to be finished and signed. They want to avoid conflict; but in doing so, they can lose jobs.

A contract is a legal, written statement that the work we do is worth something. It stipulates just how much a client is willing to pay for what we do, and how that payment will be made. It says in black and white how much an actor earns. Contracts make it clear that our work is a real job and not just a creative plaything that we don't take seriously, picking it up only when the spirit moves us.

Although the agent usually does the actual negotiating of contracts, he or she can only do what we say to do. If we're not willing to work for less than a certain amount, the agent has to honor that. The more input we give the agent, the better work he or she can do for us.

For some of us, asking for what we want is very difficult. We never learned how to do that as children, and certainly never believed that we could get a positive response. We need to make sure that the child in us is well looked after when we are talking contracts with agents; this is adult business.

When I was an agent, some clients would say, "I just want to work, I don't want to upset them by arguing about money or plane tickets. They won't want me if I do that." It was as if they were back in their dysfunctional families, where the results of asking for what they wanted were rejection and chaos.

I was always surprised at actors who would go through the agony of auditioning for a role and waiting to see whether or not they were cast, but who would then abandon themselves and their work entirely when it came time to negotiate the contract. Some were so panicked at the thought of their work becoming "real" that they couldn't even sit down and let me go over the details of the contract with them. Others said, "I want this job so badly I'd do it for nothing. Give them anything they want. I don't even care if they pay me."

These same actors would demand to know exactly what their rights were if they were buying a house, a car, or an insurance policy, but were perfectly willing to walk away from the business side of their work. They seemed to think that there was something not quite "nice" about caring about money and billing. They were often afraid it would interfere with their relationship with the director, and they would say, "Please don't do anything to lose me that job."

I loved it when actors said, "Lose it if you have to; I won't work for anything less than I got on the last job!" If the money wasn't forthcoming, they might be willing to take more in terms of billing or a higher per-diem rate, but they were not prepared to say, "I'll do anything, anything at all, just to do this job."

No one expects actors to work for free. Producers and directors have budgets and are prepared to pay for good work. They may even be willing to stretch their budgets for an artist whose work they particularly admire.

A contract frees us from nagging questions about whether and when we will be paid, about what our responsibility is to the other party, and about what his or hers is to us. This allows both of us to do our work in an atmosphere of trust and security.

Mourning the Loss of Goals Achieved

It's tempting to think that life will be better when we have achieved our goals. We imagine that if we were playing Lady Macbeth, or Antigone, then life would be wonderful indeed.

Many artists are shocked when they actually do achieve their goals and find out that instead of being elated, they feel depressed. Because an actor's career usually includes an erratic series of jobs rather than one steady climb to the top, this sense of disappointment can occur over and over again.

My client Christine, who had dreamed of playing Hedda Gabler and finally did, described the time afterward as empty. She had a sense that her bright, shining dream had deserted her. She felt directionless, as if an important part of her internal landscape had simply disappeared. In fact, it *had* disappeared. It had moved into her past, and the loss was palpable.

In such cases, the dream on which we have fixed our vision, the thing for which we have worked and sacrificed, has been achieved. Now it is behind us, rather than ahead of us. It's satisfying that we've achieved the success and realized our dream, but it's important to recognize that we've lost something in the process, and that we need to mourn the loss of that goal or dream.

Shooting is complete, the play has closed, the tour has ended. What happens tomorrow? What gets us out of bed? How do we get passionately involved in our work again?

Obviously, we need to get on with new dreams. If we don't, we may use the energy now released from the old dream in destructive ways, trying to fill up the time by abusing alcohol, drugs, or food, or by spending money we can't afford to spend. At times like these, we are more likely to act irrationally, to give in to the fear that we will never work again, and to succumb to the downward spiral of depression.

Preparing for what will happen after we have realized one of our dreams can help. We can schedule a series of new activities for just after a show closes or after some big project has been completed. We can learn to tap dance or juggle, see all the movies we've been wanting to see, go to exhibits we haven't had time to attend, and make dates with friends we haven't seen in some time. The important thing is to make sure that these activities feed us and support us through a time of mourning.

The Never-Ending Process

Our career doesn't start when we've "finished" eating the elephant; eating the elephant *is* our career. The process is what's important — the rehearsal period, the interviews, the classes, everything we do to further our work. While all these activities may culminate in a single event (such as a performance) or a specific "success" (such as an award or a job in a hit show), we must still live from day to day in the process. Our creative life is going on right now. It is not waiting out there in the future for some mythical person to signal for it to begin.

epilogue
Freeing Ourselves from the Need to Be Perfect

The compulsion to be perfect is one of the greatest impediments to eating the elephant one bite at a time and to giving ourselves permission to be just who and where we are. Many of us grew up believing that we had to be perfect but that we never could be. The frustration that results from this contradiction may be enormous.

In dysfunctional families, children often believe that if they could be perfect, their families would be perfect. The thinking goes like this: "If I could be perfect, then everything in my immediate world would be perfect too. The reason that it is *not* perfect is that I haven't tried hard enough yet. I've been working hard at it, but I'm obviously not perfect yet because the world is not perfect, and it's my fault."

This idea turns us into overachievers, but it does not turn us into good actors.

One thing the human organism cannot live without is hope. If we have grown up in a dysfunctional environment, the only way we were able to give ourselves hope was to recast the players in the drama. If we cast ourselves as the people responsible for all the chaos, if we felt responsible for it, then at least we had hope. If we had created all this trouble, perhaps we could undo it. If we could become perfect, then everything in our environment would fall into place and be perfect, too.

This is a brilliant survival technique, but eventually it catches up with us. Striving to be perfect is a judgmental function of the left brain. We know what the chattering voices of the left brain can do to us; what we need as actors is uninhibited access to the emotions and the unconscious through the right brain. We also need the involvement of the left brain in organizing it all for us, not in judging it. We need to be who we are—and we are not perfect.

We must learn to be gentle with ourselves, to give ourselves a break, to let ourselves off the hook. The whole point of this book, and of the process of overcoming creative blocks, is to learn to accept, appreciate, and express ourselves.

Webster's Ninth New Collegiate Dictionary defines "perfect" as "being entirely without fault or defect: flawless; satisfying all requirements; . . . lacking in no essential detail." These definitions create terrifying standards—standards that require or imply external judgment.

Perfection, as a goal for us as actors, excludes our most valuable asset, ourselves as we are: flawed and different from anyone else; full of dreams, full of fear, full of uncertainty, but most of all profoundly committed to the struggle to communicate. We are none of us perfect, but we are endlessly, uniquely fascinating. For an actor, perfection is not the goal. The goal is to live truthfully and honestly in the reality of each moment.

On the journey to that goal, we need to allow ourselves to express whatever we have inside, without editing it, without trying to make it perfect, whether it comes out in bright, broad, uninhibited strokes or in shadowy, ephemeral washes of color that are barely perceptible. Editing comes later; we first have to welcome that initial flash, without really knowing what we're giving birth to. Whatever it is, it is ours alone. We can work on it, shape it, throw it out altogether, or embrace it as if it were life itself. But first we have to let it happen.